The Assassination of Abraham Lincoln

An Illustrated Account of America's First Murdered President

Caleb Jenner Stephens

Published by Willow Manor Publishing
Fredericksburg, VA 22406
www.willowmanorpublishing.com
Copyright © 2015 by Caleb Jenner Stephens
All rights reserved

Cover and interior design courtesy of MS Illustration and Design

Images and illustrations found within are credited to the Library of Congress or National Archives unless otherwise noted

First published 2015
Manufactured in the United States
Includes bibliographical references.
ISBN 978-1-939688-71-2

Notice: The information in this book is true and complete to the best of our knowledge. It is offered without guarantee on the part of the author or Willow Manor Publishing. The author and Willow Manor Publishing disclaim all liability in the connection with the use of this book. All rights reserved. No part of this book may be reproduced or transmitted in any form whatsoever without prior written permission from the publisher except in the case of brief quotations embodied in critical articles and reviews.

Contents

Introduction	1
Oh Captain, My Captain - Walt Whitman	3
1 The Beginning of the End	5
2 Cabinet Meeting & Booth's Preparations	15
3 The Conspiracy	21
4 The Assassination	33
5 Lincoln's Last Night	61
6 Search for the Murderer	79
7 The Conspirators' Trial	97
Conclusion	121
References	125

INTRODUCTION

After writing *Worst Seat in the House*, a book about the life of Henry Rathbone and how the Lincoln Assassination affected him, I quickly learned how little the public knew about Lincoln's death. Many people I talked with had basic knowledge and understood the fundamental details, such as the location of Ford's Theatre and that John Wilkes Booth committed the murder. Beyond these principal facts, however, many of these people overlooked some of the most interesting details or, worse, possessed incorrect knowledge of the event. After discussing the assassination a little further I saw their eyes light with excitement and they were captivated. They thirsted for more details and I completely understood the enchantment of the tragedy. This same feeling engulfed me as a teenage boy.

While there are several wonderful and lengthy books devoted to the assassination of Abraham Lincoln, by scholars like Harold Holzer, Edward Steers Jr., and Michael Kauffman, my hope was to provide a quick, high-level overview that readers could digest rapidly. I intended to pack all the details possible in a brief assessment. Then, any readers who hungered for more would be able to move on to more comprehensive and meticulous tomes.

The Assassination of Abraham Lincoln: An Illustrated Account of America's First Murdered President touches on the whole story of assassination day, the hunt for John Wilkes Booth, and the trial of the conspirators. It highlights all the capital aspects of each portion. But there is much to discuss about the events of the assassination and this book is a primer for those who desire to dig deeper. It's also a suitable compendium for those who simply wish to study the whole tragedy in a quick fashion.

I have been fascinated with the Lincoln assassination and the characters involved for decades. The history never gets old and new information and theories seem to pop up every couple of years. I hope you become as intrigued as I and thousands of others have with the story of the first murdered American President. The sadness, horror, and drama is all at once thrilling, deceiving, and fascinating with a flurry of other emotions along the way.

O Captain! My Captain!
by Walt Whitman

O Captain! My Captain! our fearful trip is done;
The ship has weather'd every rack, the prize we sought is won;
The port is near, the bells I hear, the people all exulting,
While follow eyes the steady keel, the vessel grim and daring:
But O heart! heart! heart!
  O the bleeding drops of red,
    Where on the deck my Captain lies,
      Fallen cold and dead.

O Captain! My Captain! rise up and hear the bells;
Rise up—for you the flag is flung—for you the bugle trills;
For you bouquets and ribbon'd wreaths—for you the shores a-crowding;
For you they call, the swaying mass, their eager faces turning;
Here captain! dear father!
  This arm beneath your head;
    It is some dream that on the deck,
      You've fallen cold and dead.

My Captain does not answer, his lips are pale and still;
My father does not feel my arm, he has no pulse nor will;
The ship is anchor'd safe and sound, its voyage closed and done;
From fearful trip, the victor ship, comes in with object won;
Exult, O shores, and ring, O bells!
  But I, with mournful tread,
    Walk the deck my captain lies,
      Fallen cold and dead.

Walt Whitman wrote "O Captain! My Captain!" in reaction to the death of Abraham Lincoln. Published on November 4, 1865 in the *Saturday Press*, the poem was immediately well received as it echoed the feelings of many people at the time. Whitman was forty-six at the time of Lincoln's death and, as can be seen, was deeply impacted by the President's passing.

Chapter 1
THE BEGINNING OF THE END

The morning of April 14, 1865 gave no foreboding moments or clues that foreshadowed the night's impending tragedy. In fact, Abraham Lincoln and the people of Washington were in great spirits. The day before, the city held a Grand Illumination to celebrate the Civil War coming to an end. Windows gleamed bright with candlelight, bonfires lit up street corners, and fireworks exploded in celebration over Lafayette Square. America could see the turning point of the war and the South would soon be reunited with the North. Revelers saw Abraham Lincoln's ultimate goal on the horizon. The Union would be whole once more.

Lincoln's morning began like many others over the last four years. Rising early, somewhere around seven o'clock, President Lincoln started the day working in his office. Reviewing letters and making plans for the day, he determined a cabinet meeting was necessary to discuss the recent events and how to properly outline the end of the war. Pointedly, Lincoln wished to discuss tactics for reconstruction of the South. This signaled that his mind was indeed moving forward from the war. His focus could now shift to tending to the wounds every American felt, Northerners and Southerners. In addition, General Ulysses S. Grant was visiting Washington, so Lincoln requested his attendance at the cabinet meeting.

Around an hour later, Abraham Lincoln enjoyed breakfast with his entire family. Robert Todd Lincoln, a Captain in General Grant's Army of the Potomac, arrived home only a few days prior, and joined his father along with Mary Todd and Tad Lincoln for the morning meal. Robert, the president's oldest son, recently returned from Appomattox where he was witness to General Robert E. Lee's surrender of the Army of Northern Virginia. As the family dined, Robert regaled the President, his mother, and young brother with his recollection of the historic day. Mary Todd and twelve year old Tad, listened in earnest to Robert's account of Lee's Surrender. This momentous occasion marked a major closing point of the war.

> DID YOU KNOW?
> Sneaking into Washington
> -The Baltimore Plot
>
> As Abraham Lincoln approached Washington D.C. on his inaugural train journey, an alleged plot to assassinate the soon to be President was discovered. Evidence and rumors showed that Lincoln was to be killed passing through Baltimore, MD. Reacting to this news, Lincoln's security team, headed by Allan Pinkerton, canceled the scheduled stops in Harrisburg, PA and Baltimore, MD. Under the cover of night, the train carrying Lincoln traveled directly to Washington, where the President was escorted to the Willard Hotel.

In addition to the discussion of Lee's Surrender, Mary discussed the evening's plans and entertainment. Mary, already in possession of tickets and a reservation for the production of *Aladdin! Or The Wonderful Lamp* at Grover's Theatre, instead wished to see *Our American Cousin*

The Lincoln Family- Robert, Willie, Abraham, Mary Todd, and Tad

Credit: Library of Congress, Rare Book and Special Collections Division, Alfred Whital Stern Collection of Lincolniana

at Ford's Theatre. Lincoln agreed with Mary and they decided that Tad would attend the performance at Grover's to represent the Lincoln family. In light of the change, Mary mentioned to her husband that she hoped General Grant and his wife, Julia, would still accompany them for the night's outing.

President Lincoln offered the invitation to the distinguished couple earlier in the week. In the moment, General Grant accepted the invitation. Grant planned to work through the week and intended to still be in Washington Friday evening. However, his intentions changed after wrapping up his work early and desiring to visit his family in New Jersey. The long war had taken a toll on the General and he was looking forward to a break and seeing his children. Grant concerted on alerting the President of the change in plans at the upcoming cabinet meeting.

President Abraham Lincoln and his generals after Antietam, 1862.

After breakfast and before the cabinet meeting, Lincoln found time to meet with a few visitors. Among them was Speaker of the House Schuyler Colfax. The two men discussed ideas and concerns of Southern Reconstruction and President Lincoln also offered an invitation to Speaker Colfax to join them at Ford's Theatre. Colfax, however, was leaving for the west coast the next day and needed to prepare for his travel.

During this time, President Lincoln remembered he must alert Ford's Theatre of their arrival. He sent a messenger to

General Ulysses S. Grant.

The Beginning of the End

> ☞ **LIEUT. GENERAL GRANT, PRESIDENT** and **Mrs. Lincoln** have secured the State Box at Ford's Theater TO NIGHT, to witness Miss Laura Keene's American Cousin. It
>
> ☞ **DAWSON LODGE. No. 16.**—There will be a called meeting of Dawson Lodge. No. 16.

Announcement of President Lincoln and General Grant's attendance at Ford's Theatre in the *National Intelligencer*.

> **DID YOU KNOW?**
> **Robert Lincoln in Grant's Army**
>
> After graduating from Harvard University in 1864, Robert joined the Army of the Potomac under General Ulysses S. Grant as captain in 1865. Robert was present in Appomattox to witness Lee's surrender to Grant.
>
>

Ford's and reserved the State Box for the night's performance. The message informed management that General Grant and his wife would be accompanying the Lincolns. The owners of Ford's Theatre were ecstatic upon receiving the news. Patrons did not normally attend theater performances on Good Friday so the presence of the President and General Grant would be sure to boost ticket sales. Taking advantage of the prosperous turn of events, Ford's Theatre notified the local newspapers. That evening, in the *Washington Evening Star* and *National Intelligencer*, ads announced the appearance of President Lincoln and his victorious General Grant.

A short distance away from the White House, in room 228 of the

John Wilkes Booth- Assassinated President Abraham Lincoln on April 14, 1865 at Ford's Theatre, Washington D.C.

At Pennsylvania and 6th Street, the National Hotel was the residence of John Wilkes Booth while he plotted Lincoln's assassination. The building was torn down in 1942 and today is the home of the Newseum.

National Hotel, John Wilkes Booth began his day. Booth did little to alert anyone of his impending actions that morning, as the plan had not been fully constructed. The soon-to-be assassin's mundane and ordinary tasks, consisted of a haircut and a meeting with a few friends. It's difficult for historians to be completely certain, but the details imply that the assassination plot was yet to be in motion. Lincoln made his own plans in the same moments and Booth was unaware of the opportunity arising.

While Booth made little suspicious moves, many still felt drawn to the charismatic man. Born into one of the most famous acting families in the country, Booth was the most dramatic of them all. His flair for the theatrical went beyond the stage and many of his actions in life were self-promoting or fit into his own private agenda. Well known throughout the entire United States, Washington residents anticipated and welcomed his presence.

That morning Booth met with his fiancée, Lucy Hale, as well as conspirator Michael O'Laughlen and possibly Mary Surratt. As eleven o'clock approached and President Lincoln attended the cabinet meeting at the White House, John Wilkes Booth traveled to Ford's Theatre.

Traveling the country as an actor meant Booth needed a permanent location for his mail to be sent. Ford's Theatre was that location. During this routine trip to retrieve his mail Booth discovered the President would be in the audience during the night's performance of *Our American Cousin*.

The messenger from the White House arrived moments before Booth and theater managers had begun accommodations for the President and General. In order to create the State box, they removed a partition between two balcony boxes, creating one large room capable of seating several people. Employees brought furniture and chairs into the room and draped

> ### Did You Know?
> John Wilkes Booth's Family
>
> John Wilkes Booth came from a large and well respected family of actors. Junius Brutus Booth and Mary Ann Holmes had ten children. In addition to John Wilkes, his brothers Edwin and Junius Jr. were also famous actors. Of them all, Edwin was the most successful and regarded as one of the greatest actors of the time.
>
>
> Junius Booth, in theatrical costume.
>
>
> Edwin Booth as Hamlet.

> **DID YOU KNOW?**
> Soldier Exchange
>
> Many believe that General Grant was at fault for halting the prisoner exchange. However, the exchange stoppage officially began with General Orders 252, issued by Lincoln on July 30, 1863. At this time, Grant was only an army commander and had little input on these decisions. Grant was not fully innocent however, as he was later in charge of the prisoner of wars and failed to resume the exchange agreement in full.

American and treasury guard flags over the balcony railing.

After hearing the news of Lincoln's attendance, Booth's mind erupted with ideas. Before this day, he conspired with a group of southern sympathizers to kidnap President Lincoln. The group consisted of Lewis Powell, John Surratt, Mary Surratt, David Herold, George Atzerodt, Samuel Arnold, and Michael O'Laughlen. Booth stood as the leader and driving force of the group. They intended to kidnap Lincoln on route from the White House to the Soldier's Home. This twelve room cottage, three miles outside of Washington, served as a vacation home for the president. Lincoln and his family regularly traveled the short distance to relax, enjoy more privacy, and escape a little summer heat. The conspirators planned to take Lincoln to Richmond and then exchange him for Confederate prisoners of war. They devised the kidnapping plot months before the assassination in late 1864. At the time, complications halted the prisoner exchange and the conspirators saw their plan as the best way to help the South.

Lincoln traveled to the Soldier's Home quite often and many times he took the trip alone. This all changed, however, in August 1864 after Lincoln, on horseback, rode late at night alone. Upon nearing his destination, a gunshot rang out and startled Lincoln's horse. The President fought to stay on the spooked steed, lost his hat in the commotion, then regained control, and continued the short trip to the home. Later that night Lincoln discussed the incident with Ward Hill Lamon and the guards on duty. He made light of the situation and asked that nothing be spoken of it. But the guards thereafter discovered Lincoln's hat in the field with a bullet hole in it and Lincoln's future trips consisted of travel by carriage with armed guards.[1]

The Soldier's Home- A national monument today, the Lincoln family used the home during the warmer months of the year and to escape the pressure of politics and visitors.

Over several months, through 1864 and early 1865, the plot to kidnap Abraham Lincoln fell apart. The exchange of prisoners of war recommenced in January 1865 and Lincoln was now guarded on his trips to the Soldier's home. Despite these changes, Booth still boiled with hate and held a deep need to boost the cause of the South. Due to Booth's contempt for Lincoln and desire to be a catalyst for change in the war, the conspirators still met frequently, but the meetings became more sporadic by spring 1865. The motives and eagerness of the group faded. Booth, however, was intent on Lincoln paying for the unjust turmoil he felt the President placed on the Confederacy.

Back at Ford's Theatre, the fortuitous information of Lincoln's upcoming attendance was precisely what Booth needed and there was no time to waste. Dashing away from the theater, the zealous actor immediately began forming a plan and setting the pieces in place for his last performance.

Chapter 2
CABINET MEETING & BOOTH'S PREPARATIONS

At eleven o'clock, the cabinet meeting began in the President's office inside the White House. The present members included Secretary of War Edwin Stanton, Attorney General Joshua Speed, Secretary of the Navy Gideon Welles, Secretary of the Treasury Hugh McCulloch, and Assistant Secretary of the State Frederick Seward. Frederick's father and Secretary of State, William Seward, could not attend, being bedridden at home with terrible injuries developed from a carriage accident a few days earlier. General Grant also attended the day's meeting.

 The discussion focused on Reconstruction of the South and how to restore the country with the war finally coming to an end. According to Seward, the discourse was "long and earnest, with little diversity of opinion."[2] In addition to the rehabilitation colloquy, President Lincoln asked General Grant to speak on the surrender of Lee's Army at Appomattox. Grant briefly relayed the events of April 9th to the cabinet

Did You Know?
Lincoln's Dream

According to Ward Hill Lamon, President Lincoln discussed a dream he had a few days before the assassination. "Before me was a catafalque, on which rested a corpse wrapped in funeral vestments. Around it were stationed soldiers who were acting as guards; and there was a throng of people, gazing mournfully upon the corpse, whose face was covered, others weeping pitifully. 'Who is dead in the White House?' I demanded of one of the soldiers, 'The President,' was his answer; 'he was killed by an assassin.' Then came a loud burst of grief from the crowd, which woke me from my dream. I slept no more that night; and although it was only a dream, I have been strangely annoyed by it ever since."

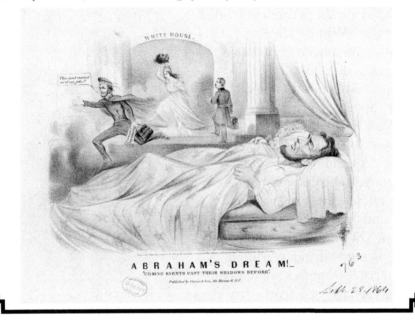

members and at approximately two o'clock the assembly adjourned.

Lincoln often shared personal stories and a recurring dream became a final topic of examination at the cabinet meeting. Only later would this dream become relevant or even prophetic. As written by Gideon Welles, Lincoln's dream involved floating in a vessel of some sort, over water, and moved "with great rapidity towards an indefinite shore."[3] Lincoln stated that the dream presented itself before every

Cabinet Meeting & Booth's Preparations

major turning point of the war. At the time, the officials awaited word from General Sherman, whose troops still fought in the South, and Lincoln supposed the vision was a sign that word would soon come of Sherman's success. After the assassination, many cabinet members related Lincoln's dream to his murder.

As the men excused themselves, President Lincoln questioned Grant if he planned to accompany him to the evening's theater performance. The General informed Lincoln of his need to decline the offer, as his plans had changed. He scheduled to board a train for New Jersey at six o'clock that evening. Grant and his wife were eager to see their children and the General completed his work early, allowing him to leave ahead of schedule.

Lincoln visited the War Department soon after the end of the cabinet meeting. The President often dropped by the War Department as it was located directly adjacent to the White House, where the Old Executive Office building stands today. It also served as the major hub of war news and telegraph dispatches. In addition to being informative, the hustling of Secretary of War Stanton's large workforce made the trips entertaining and sociable.

On the 14th, however, Lincoln intended to offer a Ford's Theatre invitation to Secretary Stanton. The Secretary immediately declined. He expressed his concern about rumors of an assassination attempt on the President's life and warned Lincoln that attending an event at such a public place could be dangerous. Lincoln brushed off Stanton's warnings though and turned his attention instead to assistant secretary of war and telegraph Superintendent Thomas Eckert.

In Stanton's previous conversation with Lincoln, he advised the Commander in Chief that if he wouldn't listen to his counsel on not attending the theater, then he should at least take a bodyguard along. In response to this President Lincoln announced,

"Stanton, do you know that Eckert can break a poker over his arm?"

The secretary responded surprisingly, "No; why do you ask such a question?"

"Well, Stanton, I have seen Eckert break five pokers, one after the

An early campaign portrait of Republican presidential candidate Abraham Lincoln.

Cabinet Meeting & Booth's Preparations

other, over his arm, and I am thinking he would be the kind of man to go with me this evening. May I take him?"

Stanton declined, stating Eckert had too much work to complete before the close of day. The secretary was doing all he could to dissuade Lincoln from attending the theater. To concede for the powerful Eckert to accompany Lincoln, would only embolden the President.

Lincoln didn't like Stanton's response and decided to ask Eckert in person. He walked into the cipher-room where Eckert worked and announced the

Thomas Eckert.

night's plans to attend *Our American Cousin* at Ford's Theatre. The President requested Eckert to join Mrs. Lincoln and himself, but in fairness stated that Stanton had already denied the request, noting the important work to be done.

Knowing the intentions of his boss, Eckert politely declined the offer. Lincoln accepted with understanding and left the War Department.[4]

Out in the streets of Washington, Booth furiously scurried about. He darted from location to location, putting things in order to ensure his success that night. He first rented a horse for escape from the city. Around noon, at a stable on C Street, Booth found a suitable steed and advised the stablehand he would return at four in the evening to retrieve it.

Around the close of the Cabinet Meeting, near two o'clock, Booth met with Lewis Powell at the Herndon House. Powell was a young, strong associate of Booth's and had been involved in the kidnapping conspiracy from almost the beginning. Powell rented a room at the Herndon House at 900 F Street around the corner from Ford's Theatre and there Booth informed him of the assassination plot. Booth told Powell of the stroke of luck they received with the President's upcoming attendance of Ford's Theatre.

> **ASSASSINATION QUESTIONS**
>
> **Was the Confederacy involved in the plot to kill Abraham Lincoln?**
>
> While no hard evidence exists, many theorists and researchers believe John Wilkes Booth was a part of a plan coordinated by the southern Confederate government. As evidence, they point to the trips Booth took to Montreal, Canada, just prior to the assassination, where a large number of Confederates soldiers and officials were stationed.

John Wilkes Booth's contrivance would be a multi-pronged attack and he needed Powell's assistance. In Booth's mind, the scheme would strike a major blow to the North in one night and turn the tide of Civil War back to the favor of the Confederates.

Chapter 3
THE CONSPIRACY

The plan devised by John Wilkes Booth not only involved killing Abraham Lincoln, but included murdering Vice President Andrew Johnson and Secretary of State William Seward in the same night. He intended to dismantle the top tier of the United States government and remove the major decision makers in one motion. With Abraham Lincoln and William Seward dead, Booth foresaw the North being thrown into a state of confusion, allowing the Confederacy a chance to overtake an unprepared enemy. He scheduled everything to take place a little after ten PM— Lincoln's death was eight hours away.

After meeting with Lewis Powell and filling him in on the newly formed plan, Booth made a brief stop at the Surratt boarding house on H Street. Mary Surratt, the owner and keeper of the boarding house also owned a tavern, approximately thirteen miles away in Surrattsville, MD. The town, today known as Clinton, had been named when Mary's late husband, John H. Surratt, was appointed postmaster. John Surratt passed away three years prior, forcing Mary to rent out rooms in her home for money.

On April 14, Booth needed Mary to take a package to her tavern. The nondescript parcel given to Surratt contained simply a pair of binoculars and she left later that day to deliver it for safe keeping with John Lloyd. Lloyd ran the tavern and leased it from Mrs. Surratt.

In addition to dropping off the package, Surratt left a message with Lloyd. According to Lloyd's later testimony, she asked him to have a set of rifles, ammunition, and the binoculars ready to be picked up that same night. Conspirator David Herold hid the weapons she spoke of inside the tavern a few weeks earlier. The accomplices originally intended the rifles to be used as part of the Lincoln kidnapping plot, but now they scheduled to pick them up during their escape after killing the President, Vice President, and Secretary of State.

John Wilkes Booth next stopped at the Kirkwood House. Vice President Andrew Johnson resided at the Kirkwood House, a hotel on Pennsylvania Avenue, and co-conspirator George Atzerodt had also recently booked a room there. Booth intended to discuss the murder of the Vice President with Atzerodt and give him the charge of killing Johnson. Neither Andrew Johnson nor Atzerodt were in at the time however, and in a peculiar move, John Wilkes Booth left a message for the Vice President with the hotel desk clerk. The note read, "Don't wish to disturb you. Are you at home? J. Wilkes Booth." The true purpose of Booth leaving the memo has never been understood.

At four o'clock, Booth returned to the stable as promised to pick up his horse. Then, after traveling to Grover's Theater and getting a drink from Deery's, a tavern above Grover's, he wrote his confession. The letter explained the conspirator's rationalizations for killing Abraham Lincoln, Andrew Johnson, and William Seward. Once completed, Booth sealed the envelope and addressed it to the *National Intelligencer*, a local Washington newspaper. He signed not only his own name, but also included the names of Lewis Powell, George Atzerodt and

> **ASSASSINATION QUESTIONS**
>
> **Why did John Wilkes Booth leave his calling card for Vice President Johnson?**
>
> This handwritten note from John Wilkes Booth to Vice President Johnson still confuses historians today. It's not quite sure what Booth's motive was for leaving the message. The card reads, "Don't wish to disturb you. Are you at home? J. Wilkes Booth."
>
>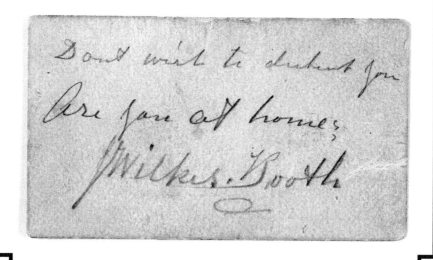

David Herold. By signing their names, Booth cemented their fates and implicated them in the murder plans in addition to the conspiracy plot.

Instead of delivering the proclamation personally, Booth gave it to a friend, fellow actor John Mathews. Mathews was to perform in the upcoming evenings show at Ford's Theatre and John Wilkes Booth passed by Mathews on the street by the Willard hotel. Booth asked Mathews to take the letter to the newspaper on April 15, 1865, the next day.

The 17th President of the United States, Andrew Johnson. Abraham Lincoln's Vice President at time of assassination.

The Conspiracy 25

The letter never made it to the *National Intelligencer*. Later, amidst the ensuing confusion, Mathews read the confession while locked inside Ford's Theatre with the rest of actors. The search for the conspirators had begun and the actors and stagehands at Ford's were confined to the theater. He knew John Wilkes Booth well, and after witnessing his escape from the stage that night, Mathews opened the letter and found it detailed Booth's reasons for murdering the President. In fear of being implicated in the conspiracy, Mathews burned the letter and spoke nothing of it until he testified in 1867 during the impeachment trial of President Andrew Johnson.[5]

With the night closing in, Booth continued his preparation with a sharp wit, despite the hurried pace. Around six in the evening he rode his horse back to Ford's Theatre and practiced the route he planned on using that night to kill the President. He only lacked the ability to rehearse jumping onto the stage from the State box balcony.

After his walkthrough and prepping at the theater, Booth invited a few of the actors and employees for a drink next door at the Star Saloon. The crew invited included stagehand Edman "Ned" Spangler. Although no evidence supported him being involved in the prior kidnapping conspiracy meetings, Spangler soon became a suspect in the murder of President Lincoln. In just a couple hours the Commander in Chief would arrive at Ford's.

In the early evening, after the cabinet meeting, Abraham Lincoln enjoyed lunch with his wife Mary and tended to some paperwork and matters awaiting attention in his office. It's thought during this time Mary found out that the Grant's would not be accompanying them to Ford's Theatre and they needed to find alternates.

At close to the same time Booth left his message at the Kirkwood House, Vice President Johnson met with Lincoln at the White House. Their meeting only lasted approximately twenty minutes, but it was the first time the Vice President met with his leader since their inauguration on March 3, 1865. Their discussion revolved around the major topic of the day, Southern Reconstruction, and the best way to deal with the traitors.

Lincoln continued meeting visitors until his official work completed a little after four o'clock. Mary Todd requested a carriage ride with her husband before dinner and Abraham happily agreed. She later recalled, in a letter to a friend, how merry the President seemed during the outing. She noted this to Lincoln and the President responded he felt happy the war was ending and stated, "We must both be more cheerful in the future - between the war and the loss of our darling Willie - we have both been very miserable."

The couple's course took them to the Navy Yard, a frequent location for Lincoln visits. The President often traveled to this area to visit with the soldiers and see the new advancements in weaponry. That day they took a tour of the U.S.S. Montauk, a monitor, or warship, used

Monitor ship U.S.S. Montauk on the right next to the U.S.S. Lehigh.

Soldiers standing near cannons at the Washington Navy Yard.

by the navy during the Civil War. In an odd twist, the vessel would soon become the ship employed to hold the prisoners and conspirators involved in Lincoln's death.

After their visit to the Navy Yard, Abraham and Mary Todd enjoyed the carriage ride back to the White House and the President entertained a few more visitors for the evening. A little after six o'clock the Lincoln family sat together for dinner. Some believe during dinner Mary informed Abe that Major Henry Rathbone and Clara Harris would be joining them at Ford's Theatre that night. They were scheduled to pick up the young couple at eight PM from the home of New York Senator Ira Harris, not far away on H Street.

Clara Harris' father, Senator Ira Harris, was also Henry Rathbone's stepfather. Henry and Clara's parents married when the two were young children, after both of their respective partners passed away a few months apart. Despite their relation by marriage, Clara and Henry had been engaged to be married themselves. At the time, Clara was thirty-one years old and Henry Rathbone was twenty-eight.

Did You Know?
Mary Todd Lincoln

Born in 1818 and married to Abraham Lincoln in 1842, Mary lived seventeen years after the assassination, dying in 1882 at the age of sixty-two. Mary was a complicated figure during her four years in Washington, but was a staunch supporter of her husband and his policies.

DID YOU KNOW?
Other Invitations

General Grant wasn't the only person to decline the Lincoln's invitation to Ford's Theatre. Before Henry Rathbone and Clara Harris accepted, there were between twelve to fifteen other invitations declined. After learning that Grant and his wife Julia would not be attending, Lincoln and Mary Todd invited Robert Todd Lincoln, Schuyler Colfax, Secretary of War Stanton, Thomas Eckert, Noah Brooks, the Marquis de Chambrun, and a few others throughout the day. Obviously, they all turned down the First Couple and missed the fateful meeting with history.

The invitation for Clara wasn't out of the ordinary as Mary Todd Lincoln frequently invited her to visit. A few days prior, she paid a call to the White House to watch Lincoln give a speech from an upstairs window to a crowd down below. John Wilkes Booth happened to be in the crowd that night listening and it's rumored he became enraged as

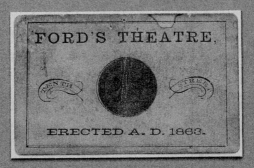

The Conspiracy

Ford's Theatre- 10th Street Washington D.C.

> **DID YOU KNOW?**
> Clara and Henry's parents died 3 days apart
>
> Henry Rathbone's father, Jared Rathbone, passed away on May 13, 1845, while Clara Harris' mother, Louisa Tubbs Harris, May 18, 1845. This allowed their widowed mother and father to marry three years later making them step-siblings.

President Lincoln spoke of giving black men the right to vote.

The interesting part about this invitation of Clara and Henry is the number of people solicited before them and how many declined. The exact total varies depending on sources, but it's estimated that between thirteen and fifteen acquaintances turned down invitations before Clara and Henry accepted. Unfortunately for the young couple, it would be a night that severely affected the rest of their lives.

> **DID YOU KNOW?**
> Ward Hill Lamon
>
> Lamon was a close friend and unofficial bodyguard of Abraham Lincoln. From 1861 through 1865, Lamon served as U.S. Marshall for the District of Columbia and took the safety and well-being of President Lincoln very seriously. Lamon, a very large and imposing figure, was a part of the group that snuck Lincoln into D.C. before the inauguration. Unfortunately, he was not present the night of the assassination, as Lincoln sent Lamon to Richmond, V.A. on business.

After dinner, the President met with two more associates. First, Speaker of the House Schuyler Colfax and then Congressman George Ashmun. A little after eight o'clock in the evening Lincoln finally broke free from his visitors. A carriage already waited in front of the White House for departure with coachman Francis P. Burke and the President's valet Charles Forbes.

President Lincoln and Mary Todd entered the carriage and after a short ride stopped at the residence of Senator Ira Harris, where Henry Rathbone and Clara Harris joined the Presidential couple. Ford's Theatre was only a few blocks away from the Harris home and at approximately 8:30 the party arrived.

Charles Forbes jumped from his post on the carriage to open the door and Ford's Theatre doorman John M. Buckingham and a police officer, John Parker, met the party. They then led the presidential group of four into the theater.

Chapter 4
THE ASSASSINATION

As the killing hour drew closer, John Wilkes Booth arrived back in his room at the National Hotel and began preparing supplies for the night's attack. He changed into all black, including coat, pants, hat, and boots with new spurs. Inside his pants he tucked a seven inch hunting dagger, then filled his pockets with a compass and his diary.

Picking up the .44 caliber Philadelphia derringer, Booth carefully loaded a lead ball into the gun. The derringer was a single shot pistol and a misfire would be a disaster to his plan,  which is why he also carried the dagger. This backup could help to fend off any other attackers or stab the President if necessary.

Near eight o'clock, as President Lincoln prepared to leave for Ford's Theatre, Booth left the National Hotel and made his way to the last meeting with conspirators Lewis Powell, David Herold, and George Atzerodt. The plan was fairly simple, but even a minor issue may derail the efforts.

John Wilkes Booth's Compass which was used during his escape after shooting President Lincoln.

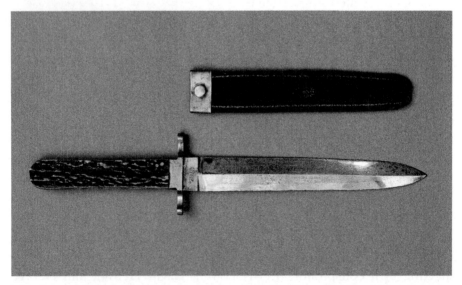

The dagger used by John Wilkes Booth to stab Major Henry Rathbone after shooting Abraham Lincoln.

The Assassination

The Philadelphia derringer used by John Wilkes Booth to assassinate Abraham Lincoln. The .44 caliber pistol could fire only one round before being loaded again.

At approximately 10:15 PM, they intended to carry out all three attacks simultaneously. After completing their deadly tasks they decided they should meet at the Navy Yard Bridge and escape into Maryland. Lewis Powell was to murder Secretary of State William Seward at his home in Lafayette Square. Some evidence suggests Powell wasn't clear on the directions to Seward's home, so they assigned David Herold the role of guide. Herold needed to get Powell to Seward's house, then help him escape after he completed the assassination of Secretary Seward. Herold's extensive knowledge of the area would make him a valuable asset as a guide.

The group assigned Atzerodt to assassinate Vice President Johnson at the Kirkwood House, but Atzerodt disapproved of this change in plans. According to later testimony, Atzerodt explained he didn't want to be a part of the murders, he only ever expected to be involved with the kidnapping plot. Booth advised Atzerodt and the other conspirators they could not back out at that point. He made it clear their involvement up to this point would implicate them regardless. He also warned their deaths would be imminent should they be caught and they had no choice but to follow their new course. Booth demanded the new plan must be followed through with and left Atzerodt and the others thinking they had settled the matter. But Atzerodt still felt unsure of his assignment. In his mind, the conspiracy took an unexpected menacing turn and George was afraid.

John Wilkes Booth assigned the President to himself. He wanted to kill Abraham Lincoln. Booth's flair for the dramatic and his desperate desire to be the star of the show allowed for no other way. In his dysfunctional mind, Booth wanted his name to be synonymous with the heroes who came before him, the men that brought down tyrants and saved an oppressed people. Booth wanted his name alone tied to the death of President Lincoln.

The exterior of Ford's Theatre. The Star Saloon is immediately to the right of the Theatre.

John Wilkes Booth, date unknown.

Inside Ford's Theatre, Abraham Lincoln, Mary Todd, Clara Harris, and Henry Rathbone enjoyed *Our American Cousin* from the second floor balcony State box. The theater consisted of three levels in total, the first floor or orchestra level, the dress circle, and then the third floor or family circle. From the vantage point of the stage, the State box was located on the left hand side, opposite from the Ford's Theatre entrance.

To access the box, one would have to walk the entire span of the dress circle level, which the President and his entourage completed earlier in the night. As they passed unknowingly through the back, actress Laura Keene noticed Abraham Lincoln, stopped the performance, and adlibbed a Presidential announcement. In response, the crowd spun to face the regal party and offered a standing ovation to their great leader as the orchestra banged out an impromptu version of *Hail to the Chief*. Laura Keene was the star of the show and lead actress playing the part of Florence Trenchard that night. In fact, that night's performance was billed as a "benefit and last night for Miss Laura Keene." This meant the house proceeds of that night's show would go to her.

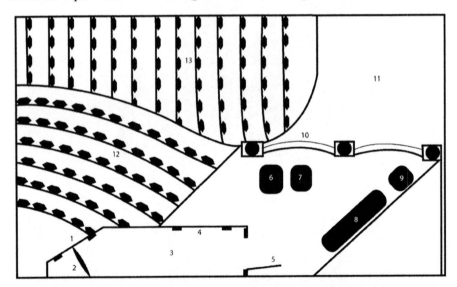

1. Booth's entry 2. The bar blocking the entry door 3. The vestibule 4. Door 7 5. Door 8 6. Abraham Lincoln 7. Mary Todd Lincoln 8. Henry Rathbone 9. Clara Harris 10. Railing Booth leapt over 11. The Stage 12. Dress Circle 13. Orchestra level seats

Interior of the box at Ford's Theatre. Abraham Lincoln was seated in the chair on the far left.

An outer door in the main dress circle area opened into a small hallway which could be considered a vestibule. After entering the vestibule, two more doors blocked entry into the box. The State box which occupied the Presidential party was actually two different boxes turned into one. To create a more grand seating area for the President, Ford's managers had removed a partition wall between the two boxes. For this reason, two doors led into the large box from the outside vestibule at the time. The door from the dress circle, however, was the only entrance into the hallway.

President Lincoln sat closest to the entrance of the State box, in a wooden rocking chair, near the balustrade of the balcony. Lincoln moved very little throughout the night, but some reports mention him standing at one point during the show to put on his coat after feeling chilled. Besides this, nothing much noteworthy occurred prior to

The rocking chair that Abraham Lincoln sat in when John Wilkes Booth attacked.

John Wilkes Booth's arrival. Lincoln could barely be seen by the patrons below, but the audience craned their necks and stretched as far as possible to catch a glimpse of the sixteenth President of the United States.

The crowd also expected to catch a glimpse of General Grant, however they found Major Henry Rathbone, a man unknown to most, in his stead. Rathbone sat on the far side of the State box, opposite Lincoln and the box door. He found himself relegated to the corner, on a red velvet sofa against the back wall. To the left of Rathbone and slightly forward sat Clara Harris and in between Clara and the President perched Mary Todd.

The State box had been adorned and decorated in honor of the President's attendance. The U.S. and treasury flags were draped from the balustrade, with a framed portrait of George Washington resting on a ledge outside the box between the flags. The Lincolns sat close to each other and their

ASSASSINATION QUESTIONS

Did Laura Keene enter the state box?

A point of contention among historians and researchers is whether actress Laura Keene entered the state box the night of the assassination. While there is no certainty, some evidence describes Keene bringing water into the State box after Lincoln was shot and then cradling the Presidents head in her lap, soaking her dress in blood. Many dispute this possibility due to the number of people present and the small space of the State box. Laura Keene was also not mentioned in any of the doctor's reports from that night.

appearances suggested they enjoyed the night's outing. Mary noted her husband's delightful mood earlier in the evening and now they sat holding hands. Their affection gave Mary a bit of apprehension, evidenced by her question to Abraham,

"What will Miss Harris think of my hanging on to you so?" Lincoln simply replied, "She won't think anything about it."

Outside the State box, near the door to the hallway in the Dress Circle, Charles Forbes watched the play from seat three-hundred. As Lincoln's messenger and valet, he had been appointed the task of simply delivering any messages to the President.

John Parker, however, was appointed as the President's guard from the Metropolitan Police Force. His station should have been in the hallway vestibule between the State box and the outer seats in the Dress Circle. The location of John Parker during Booth's attack has been a leading mystery of the assassination. While Lincoln did possess a cavalier attitude concerning his security, it's unknown if the President excused Parker or not. One thought is Lincoln permitted Parker to move as he had no view of the play from inside the hallway. Other historians believe Parker simply abandoned his post and, having been known to imbibe quite often, was drinking next door at the Star Saloon.

As the Lincolns and their guests enjoyed the play inside, John Wilkes Booth approached the back alley of Ford's Theatre. He rode the horse he'd rented earlier in the day and needed someone to hold the animal and ready it for a quick escape. Booth called out for Ned Spangler, the stagehand that drank with the assassin earlier in the day, but Spangler's tasks kept him too busy for Booth's request. Inside, he worked changing scenes for the play. That mattered little to Booth and he insisted and demanded to see Spangler. Another theater employee, hearing Booth's demands, approached Spangler inside the theater and told him that Booth was waiting for him in the alley.

Leaving his scene work, Spangler walked out back where Booth requested him to hold the horse. Spangler argued that he couldn't due to his work, but Booth paid no attention to Spangler's argument, handed the stagehand the reigns, and entered the back door of the theater. Needing to get back to his job, Spangler called over Joseph "Peanuts" Burroughs and told him to hold Booth's steed. He then walked back inside and went back to work.

John Wilkes Booth entered Ford's Theatre and traveled under the stage towards Taltavull's Star Saloon. The hour neared 9:30 and the agreed upon time for the coinciding assassinations was drawing close. Booth ordered a bottle of whisky and water, undoubtedly strengthening his nerve for the upcoming task.

> ### ASSASSINATION QUESTIONS
>
> **What happened to John Parker?**
>
> It's unknown why Metropolitan Police Officer John Parker wasn't stationed in the vestibule between the State box and the door J.W. Booth entered. Either leaving with Lincoln's permission or not, Parker's record as a policeman was abhorrent. Before that night he'd been reprimanded for several infractions, including conduct unbecoming an officer, being drunk on duty, sleeping on duty, and frequenting a prostitution house.
>
> After the assassination, John Parker was charged with "Neglect of Duty" on May 1, 1865. However, the charges were dropped June 2, 1865. Despite this, in the eyes of Lincoln's friend William H. Crook and Mary Todd Lincoln, Parker was guilty of helping to murder her husband and the President would have survived if Parker did his job. John Parker was fired from the police force three years later for sleeping on duty. He died from pneumonia in 1890.

Several blocks from Ford's at the Kirkwood House, George Atzerodt had a similar idea. The clock passed ten and Atzerodt knew the plan required him to act soon. To build his courage he approached the hotel bar and began drinking. While sitting there, he questioned the bartender about the Vice President, his whereabouts and recent actions. These questions proved to be a disaster when the bartender later notified the police investigators of a man acting suspicious and asking about Vice President Johnson.

As 10:15 passed, Atzerodt lost his resolve. He couldn't bring himself to kill someone, an act they didn't discuss when he signed on for the kidnapping plot. Atzerodt left the Kirkwood House a short time later and anxiously walked the streets of Washington for the rest of the night.

In nearby Lafayette Square, across from the White House, Lewis Powell had no problems with his nerve. With David Herold as his guide, Powell strode toward the home of Secretary of State William Seward. Herold remained in the street as Powell walked to the front door and knocked. A house waiter, William Bell, answered the door and Powell notified the man that he was to deliver medicine to his employer.

Seward was recuperating from a near fatal carriage accident that occurred nine days earlier on April 5th. The secretary received several injuries from the accident, including a broken jaw that required a metal splint and brace attached to his face. When Powell arrived, Seward was in bed being tended to by his son and daughter, Frederick and Fanny Seward.

Believing Powell's lie about being a messenger from the doctor, Bell allowed him to enter the home. Powell argued that the medicine had to be delivered and administered in person, which seemed odd to Bell, but he gave in to the demand and pointed Powell up the stairs to the secretary's bedroom. Overhearing the discussion, Frederick Seward approached the assassin near the top of the stairs, before Powell reached the bedroom. Powell, once again, stated he must deliver the medicine to Secretary Seward in person, but Frederick's intuition made him suspicious of Powell and he refused to let him pass. Frederick stated that his father was asleep and could not be bothered.

Powell grew agitated and the determination to complete his assignment overcame him. Lunging at Frederick, Powell drew his pistol and pointed it at Frederick's head. In the same instant he pulled the trigger, but nothing happened. The gun misfired. Aggravated even more, Lewis Powell turned the gun and began beating Frederick on

Secretary of State William Seward - Held the office from March 5, 1861 through March 4, 1869. He was a close friend and adviser to Abraham Lincoln who previously served as a New York Senator and Governor.

the skull with the handle. David Herold noticed the altercation from outside and fled from the Seward estate.

With Frederick subdued for the moment, Powell burst into the bedroom of Secretary Seward. Fanny Seward, watching over her father, noticed the pistol in Powell's left hand and the knife in the right as he bombarded into the room. Fearing for her father's life she screamed out "Don't kill him!" as Powell lunged for his target. He stabbed at the Secretary several times around the face and neck, once piercing entirely through Seward's right cheek.

Hearing the commotion, Seward's second son Augustus and Sergeant George Robinson, an attendant of Seward, dashed into the room and began pulling at the assassin. Powell slashed with his blade and beat down with the blunt end of the knife, furiously doing as much damage as possible. Augustus called out that he was retrieving his pistol, causing Powell to break free and escape from the house. As he ran out the front door and down the street he screamed, "I'm mad! I'm mad!"

Around six blocks away, as 10:15 approached, Booth exited the saloon next door to Ford's and made his way into the theater. Passing through the same the entrance Lincoln did earlier, he creeped up the winding staircase leading to the Dress Circle and progressed, insouciant, toward the President's box. Booth was a well-known figure, not only in Washington, but the entire United States, and a few audience members caught a fleeting sight of the famous actor.

Booth stopped at one point and leaned against the back wall of the theater. He intended to wait for a specific moment in the play and he may have been ascertaining how much time remained. He soon approached Charles Forbes, sitting outside of the State box, and handed Lincoln's messenger a card. It's assumed this was simply a calling card, notifying Forbes that he wished to greet the President.

Forbes allowed Booth to enter and the assassin did so in silence. After entering, he reached out for a wooden post, the leg of a music

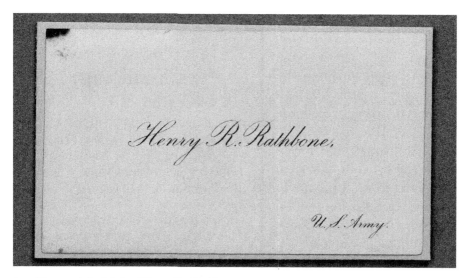

A calling card for Major Henry R. Rathbone. A card similar to this may have been what John Wilkes Booth handed to Charles Forbes before entering the State Box.

stand. With caution and without causing attention to himself, Booth jammed one end of the wooden post against the door that he just entered and the other end against the wall opposite the door. The exact time he left the leg in the vestibule hallway is still unknown, but it's assumed he found a moment during one of his earlier visits in the day.

With the only entrance to the State box barricaded, Booth ensured he would not be interrupted. The third act of *Our American Cousin*, a play that had been running for several years and one that Booth knew quite well, continued on stage. He planned to mask the sound of the gun with the laughter of the audience. A line in the script approached, that, for the time period, was known to get an uproarious reaction.

Booth moved with stealth about the outer vestibule and hid from view until the right moment. In testimony provided by Major Henry Rathbone, the door leading straight into the State box had been left open, meaning Booth needed to make small movements and stay within the shadows as much as possible. With Rathbone sitting in direct line to the entrance door, any abrupt maneuvers by Booth may have caught Rathbone's peripheral vision.

The first door in the hallway, the one used for the separate box, had a small hole drilled through to the other side. To this day, it's not certain who drilled the hole, but Booth was able to peek through and locate President Lincoln sitting in his chair. With Lincoln in position and the moment on stage drawing near, Booth prepared for his attack.

The dialogue Booth awaited would be spoken by actor Harry Hawk, playing the main character Asa Trenchard. The comedy, written by Tom Taylor, first premiered in 1858. It told the story of the ill-mannered-American Asa Trenchard who traveled to England to claim an estate from a deceased wealthy uncle. Asa's rough American ways clash with the distinguished and upscale lifestyle of many of the estate's guests. It's this dichotomy of culture that is the foundation of the play and sets up the line that John Wilkes Booth knows is seconds away.

Assassination Questions

Who drilled the hole in the door?

The identity of who drilled the hole in the State box door and purpose of the hole is still up for debate. Initially, many believed it to be drilled by John Wilkes Booth early in the day of April 14. Later, John Ford, owner of Ford's Theatre, stated he had the hole drilled to give Lincoln's guards the ability to look on the President without opening the door.

Booth clutched the .44 caliber Philadelphia derringer in his right hand and listened with intent to the play. He's just out of view of the State box guests and everything is going according to plan. On stage, Mary Wells played English mother Mrs. Mountchessington who is trying to peddle her unmarried daughters to wealthy aristocrats. She called out in disdain of Asa Trenchard, "I am aware, Mr. Trenchard, you are not used to the manners of good society, and that, alone, will excuse the impertinence of which you have been guilty."

Booth's cue had been spoken. Asa Trenchard's upcoming response will send the crowd into laughter. He steadied himself as Mrs. Mountchessington stormed off into the wings. She left Harry Hawk alone on stage. Booth turned the small corner and entered the box slowly as Asa yelled out in contempt, "Don't know the manners of good society, eh? Well, I guess I know enough to turn you inside out, old gal - you sockdologizing old man-trap."

The audience erupted in laughter and John Wilkes Booth raised the derringer pistol up to Lincoln's head. He placed the gun just behind the President's left ear and pulled the trigger. The gunshot rang out into the theatre, but the laughter of the crowd muffled the blast. The State box filled with the charge of gun smoke and Henry Rathbone, the first aware of the attack, rose from his seat.

Outside of the State box a general confusion stilted the crowd. Many were unaware anything occurred, while others figured the noise to be part of the show. Inside the box, Major Rathbone leapt from his seat to apprehend the assassin. Booth dropped the derringer and readied himself for Rathbone. They wrestled for a moment, until Booth broke free to pull the large dagger from his pants. He swiped at Rathbone with an overhand thrust. Booth aimed for Major Rathbone's chest, but the soldier parried the blow and the knife redirected into the Major's left arm. Booth dragged the knife downward, slicing a deep and long wound from the shoulder to almost the elbow, forcing Rathbone to release the assassin. He then spun toward the baluster, swept his legs over the edge, and leapt from the edge of the balcony to the stage twelve feet below.

He intended this to be an easy getaway, but Major Rathbone made one last attempt and grasped for Booth, tugging on the edge of the

THE ASSASSINATION OF PRESIDENT LINCOLN.
AT FORD'S THEATRE WASHINGTON.D.C.APRIL 14TH 1865.

One of the more famous depictions of the Lincoln assassination. As with most depictions, there are many artistic liberties, but this image is one of the most accurate, as far as placement of the individuals in the box.

assassin's coat. In addition, the treasury flag, draped along the outer edge of the State box, caused an issue for the killer. The fabric of the flag caught the new spurs on his boots as if the banner itself wished to constrain the traitor.

These two hazards caused the athletic and graceful actor to land awkwardly on the stage, as seen by a few audience members, and the plummet may have broken his leg.

Rising from the stage floor, the famous Shakespearean actor faced the crowd in the same manner he'd done thousands of times before. He lifted the blood covered dagger he stabbed Major Rathbone with high into the air and screamed out one last line on the stage.

"Sic Semper Tyrannis!"

The Latin phrase translates to "Thus Always to Tyrants." The state

The Assassination

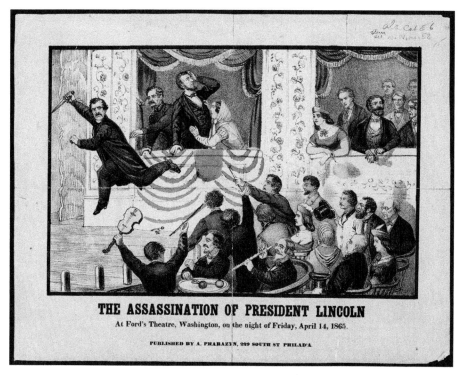

Another depiction of the Lincoln assassination. This image takes many artistic liberties and has several inaccuracies, which often leads to incorrect facts weaving into stories handed down to future generations. This image shows Lincoln standing and also emits the presence of Clara Harris. It also shows another box adjacent to the State box, full of onlookers. While there was another box on the opposite side of the stage, it was empty.

of Virginia adopted the well-known slogan as its official motto in 1776.

Booth then turned away from the audience, scurried across the stage, through the curtains, and out the back door. He burst into the alley and found his horse waiting exactly where he had left it, however now "Peanuts" Burroughs held the animal and not Ned Spangler. Booth moved with haste, snatched the reigns of the horse from Peanuts, hoisted himself into the saddle, and tore off into the night.

Major Henry R. Rathbone. Invited at the last minute, along with his fiancée Clara Harris, Rathbone was the only person to confront John Wilkes Booth after the assassination. Receiving a near fatal wound, Rathbone struggled with the trauma of that night for many years, ultimately leading to the tragedy of him murdering Clara.

The Assassination

Clara Harris, the daughter of Senator Ira Harris, was the friend of First Lady Mary Todd Lincoln and a frequent guest of the Presidential couple. Her actions on assassination night, comforting Mary Todd Lincoln and assisting with the treatment of Rathbone's knife wound, proved very heroic. Her heroism was later tested, eighteen years later, after guiding a deranged and armed Henry Rathbone away from their children. Henry shot and stabbed Clara to death minutes later.

Did You Know?

Major Rathbone and Clara Harris

Henry and Clara married two years after the assassination. They had three children and traveled Europe, but Henry was never the same after April 14, 1865. In 1883, on the morning of Christmas Eve, Henry attacked and killed Clara. He stabbed and shot her multiple times using similar weapons to the ones John Wilkes Booth brandished during the assassination. He spent the last twenty-seven years of his life in an insane asylum. Rathbone's life and the later tragedy is examined in detail in the book, *Worst Seat in the House.*

Back inside the theater, the crowd came to the realization of what took place. When John Wilkes Booth crossed the stage, Rathbone yelled out, "Stop that man!" and his fiancée Clara echoed, "Stop that man! Won't somebody stop that man?" A few men bounded on stage in pursuit, but not fast enough to apprehend Booth.

About forty feet from the State box on the second floor was Dr. Charles Leale, a twenty-three year old U.S. Army surgeon. Leale approached the door after he observed the knife in Booth's hand and heard the terrible commotion inside the President's box.

Inside the State box, Rathbone, ignoring the profuse bleeding from his arm, scanned the horrific scene. President Lincoln sat slumped in his chair, "his head was slightly bent forward and his eyes were closed." The Major read the signs and assumed Lincoln to be "mortally wounded." If anything could be done, it needed to occur now.[6]

Henry rushed to the outer door of the vestibule and pulled and pleaded with his one good arm, but the door wouldn't budge. He soon found the barricade to be "by a heavy piece of plank." The young military officer caught the sounds of men "beating against the door for the purpose of entering" but Henry couldn't move the wood lodged between the door and the wall.[7]

With his injured arm held fast against his body, the shirt sleeve and jacket soaked in blood, Henry thrust his weight against the wooden leg and dislodged the blockade. After opening the door, a sea of men presented themselves, trying to make their way into the State box. Henry wanted to protect the injured President and the two women shaken from the experience. To do this he only allowed men that "represented themselves as surgeons" to pass. The first of these surgeons was Dr. Charles Leale.[8]

Leale passed through the short outer hallway and, entering the State box, found Mary Todd Lincoln and Clara Harris "very much excited." In a later report, he stated that he first found the President "seated in a high backed arm-chair with his head leaning towards his right side supported by Mrs. Lincoln who was weeping bitterly. Miss Harris was near her left and behind the President."

Leale understood time was not on his side and began to evaluate President Lincoln to ascertain his wounds. Dr. Leale took note Lincoln was "in a state of general paralysis, his eyes were closed and he was in a profoundly comatose condition, while his breathing was intermittent and exceedingly strenuous."[9]

The young doctor continued to search for clues that might aid him in reviving Abraham Lincoln. After seeing Booth on stage with the knife and discovering Rathbone had been stabbed, Leale focused his search for a knife wound. With the help of some men that had entered the box, he had the President lowered to the floor. During this process, he supported Lincoln's head and shoulders which allowed him to discover "a large firm clot of blood" on the back of Lincoln's head.

As he inspected the area, Leale found the blood clot could be "easily removed" and he passed his little finger "through the perfectly smooth opening made by the ball." He then understood the severity of the crisis and the situation became even more dire.

Labored breathing accompanied the President's faint pulse until Leale made a significant discovery. After removing his finger from the bullet hole, "a slight oozing of blood followed" and the President's "breathing became more regular." Clearing blood clots became essential over the next several hours in the effort to improve Lincoln's condition.

Soon two other doctors in attendance at Ford's, Dr. Charles S. Taft and Dr. Albert F. A. King joined Leale in his attempt to save the dying President. Dr. Leale informed the new physicians of President Lincoln's status and the three of them soon agreed the President needed to be removed from the theater. They were certain the President would not survive this mortal wound and no one favored the idea of Lincoln dying in the playhouse. The first choice, the White House, proved to be too far from their current position. Any hope Lincoln had of survival necessitated a nearby location.

The doctors presumed a nearby home could be used and asked four soldiers standing near the door to lift Lincoln and carry him from the box. The procession, including the three doctors, Mary Todd Lincoln, Clara Harris and Henry Rathbone, made it's way through the crowd of the second floor Dress Circle. At the top of the winding staircase two other soldiers joined in carrying the President. Laying horizontal, Lincoln's body had a soldier on each leg and two at the shoulders carrying the weight of his torso. His middle section began slumping however and this is where two new volunteers took hold.

As they journeyed down the stairs towards the exit, Major Rathbone asked nearby Major Potter, an army paymaster, to accompany and assist

Dr. Charles A. Leale. The twenty-three year old Army surgeon was the first doctor at Lincoln's side after the shooting and ascertained the President's wounds.

COURIER---EXTRA.

National Calamity!

Lincoln & Seward Assassinated!!

WASHINGTON, April 15, 1865.

President Lincoln was shot through the head last night, and died this morning.— The Assassin is supposed to be Wilkes Booth the Actor. About the same time a desperado called at Secretary Seward's, pretending to be a messenger from his physician Being refused admittance, he attacked Frederick Seward, son of the Secretary, knocking down the male attendant, he cut Mr. Seward's throat, the wound was not at first considered fatal. Letters found in Booth's trunk shows that this assassination was contemplated before the fourth of March but fell through from some cause, or other. The wildest excitement prevails at Washington. Vice President's and residences of the different Secretaries are closely guarded.

LATER—Seward died this A. M. 9:45.   E. M. STANTON, Sec'y of War.

This sad intelligence falls like a dark pall on the hearts of the people so joyous and hopeful, yesterday, so terribly overwhelmed to-day. What rebels in Richmond dare not do, their accomplices and sympathizes have accomplished in our own capitol.

NOTICE.

All who abhor assassination, deplore murder, and detest the "deep damnation" of the taking off of our Chief Magistrate and Secretary of State, and who sincerely grieve for the great and good men gone are called on to meet

ON THE PUBLIC SQUARE,

AT

3 O'clock, this afternoon, April 15, 1865.

Mrs. Lincoln and Ms. Harris. The pain in his arm had intensified and coupled with the continued loss of blood he became less useful every minute. With the doctors leading the way, Lincoln emerged from the same door he entered earlier in the evening, however now the path reverberated with sobbing and confusion.

Onlookers populated from the crowd inside Ford's Theatre and passersby learning the horrific news filled Tenth Street. The three doctors looked for a respectable home for the ailing Lincoln but the task proved difficult with the curious crowd and dark street.

On the opposite side of the street, across from Ford's Theatre was the Petersen boarding house. Henry Safford, a tenant of the house, heard the disturbance and went out to see the commotion. Watching the scene, Safford realized the doctors and soldiers needed a place to bring Lincoln and called out to the men, "Bring him in here!"

The Petersen house consisted of two levels, but the narrow staircase made the second floor a poor option. Instead they chose to take Lincoln to a room in the back of the house, however the bed was too small for his six foot four inch frame. To accommodate his height, the soldiers laid the President's body diagonally along the mattress.

Chapter 5
LINCOLN'S LAST NIGHT

Several blocks from the Petersen house, Tad Lincoln cheerfully enjoyed the performance of *Aladdin! or His Wonderful Lamp!* at Grover's National Theatre. Tad sat alongside Alphonso Donn, a Metropolitan police officer and White House guard. During the performance a man entered their private box and notified Donn of the President's assassination. With haste Donn escorted Tad from the theater and after they exited, Grover's stage manager C.D. Hess announced to the rest of the crowd that President Lincoln had been shot at Ford's. Even before the official announcement, rumors started to spread among the crowd, but now, with this verification, the audience became increasingly discomposed.

Alphonso Donn waited to tell Tad about his father until after they left the theater. Tad learned of the news before arriving at the White House, where he came upon doorkeeper Thomas Pendel. The boy burst into tears when he saw Pendel and the doorkeeper wrapped the

The Petersen house: The House Where Lincoln Died - After the assassination doctors and soldiers carried the body of Abraham Lincoln to this house, located across 10th Street from Ford's Theatre. Placed in a back bedroom, the President was observed throughout the night by friends and family until passing early the next morning.

child in his arms. Tad cried out, "O Tom Pen! Tom Pen! They have killed papa dead. They've killed papa dead!"

By this time Robert Todd Lincoln already received the news and had left the White House. En route to the Peterson House, he was unaware of his father's true condition as rumors and fabrications of the truth ran rampant throughout Washington.

Robert found the Petersen house filled with soldiers, politicians, and doctors. His mother, Mary Todd, sat in the front parlor, sobbing uncontrollably. She'd been asked to wait there after peppering her husband with kisses and pleading for him to speak. Despite the assumption the President would not survive his mortal wound, the doctors had work to do, and Mary's incessant requests and sporadic movements prevented them from their periodic evaluations. Robert

Petersen House- A view from across 10th Street, standing in front of Ford's Theatre.

Petersen House: Front Parlor - After entering the Petersen house, the front parlor is the first room on the left. This is the room Mary Todd Lincoln occupied most of the night while being comforted by her son Robert.

spent the rest of the night with his mother, consoling her as best he could and sharing in her desperate tears and grief.

Lincoln lay oddly on the short bed and the doctors propped his head up with pillows. The blood from his wound soaked through and saturated the bed-sheets underneath. By eleven PM Dr. Robert King Stone, the Lincoln family physician, arrived and had been debriefed by Dr. Leale and the other physicians. From that point forward Dr. Stone held the responsibility of President Lincoln's care. He quickly completed his own examination and agreed with the other doctors that Lincoln would not recover from the wound and "that death certainly would soon close the scene."[10]

Lincoln's appearance and condition changed as the hours progressed. His right eye swelled and discolored. His extremities grew colder. His pulse rate varied throughout the evening, but ultimately

Did You Know?

Robert Todd Lincoln

The oldest of the Lincoln children, Robert was the last surviving member of the immediate family, dying in 1926 at the age of 82. After the Civil War and the assassination, Robert moved to Chicago and found success in law and politics. He served as Secretary of War under Presidents James Garfield and Chester A. Arthur. He is buried at Arlington National Cemetery.

Left to right: William Howard Taft, Warren G. Harding and Robert Todd Lincoln. Below: The tomb of Robert Todd Lincoln at Arlington Cemetary.

Did You Know?
Mary Todd Lincoln's stay in the asylum

On May 20, 1875, ten years after Lincoln's assassination and four years after Tad's death, Mary Todd was committed to Bellevue Place, a sanitarium for women. Her oldest son, Robert, began the process of having the insanity trial. His mother's behavior had grown increasingly worrisome and at the advice of doctors, he had her committed. Mary Todd's stay was short lived however. Due to her persistent letter writing and work with lawyers she was released September 11, 1875. After only four months in the asylum a Chicago court declared her officially sane.

Did You Know?

Lincoln's Children

Of the four Lincoln children, only Robert Todd Lincoln survived beyond the age of eighteen. Edward Lincoln, the second son, died of consumption at the age of 3. William "Willie" Lincoln, the third son, died of typhoid fever at the age of 11 while living in the White House. Finally, Thomas "Tad" Lincoln died at the age of 18, possibly from pneumonia or tuberculosis, six years after the assassination. Robert Todd Lincoln surpassed them all, living to the age of 82. He died in 1926 of a cerebral hemorrhage.

On the left: Tad Lincoln
On the right: Willie and Tad Lincoln with their cousin Lockwood Todd.

weakened and Dr. Stone found it difficult to note at certain points. According to M.B. Field, Assistant Secretary of the Treasury, Lincoln's breathing was regular, "but with effort, and did not seem to be struggling or suffering."[11]

Near the same time the soldier's and doctors carried Lincoln's body to the Petersen house, John Wilkes Booth arrived at the Navy Yard bridge on the outer edge of the city. The bridge, adjacent to the Navy Yard, crossed the Anacostia River and was one of the few exits out of Washington towards Southern Maryland. Booth's escape plan began with a visit to Mary Surratt's tavern in Surrattsville, Maryland, approximately ten miles from the bridge.

That night, U.S. Army Sergeant Silas T. Cobb guarded the Navy Yard bridge and the standing order for the entire city was no entry or exit from Washington after nine PM But with the war nearing its end, Sgt. Cobb seemed lax on those rules. When John Wilkes Booth appeared, the soldier questioned the assassin on his destination and why he traveled so late at night. Booth informed the man he was simply heading home and thought it best to wait until late at night so that he could use the bright moonlight to see better. Sgt. Cobb found nothing distrustful about Booth and let him pass.

A few minutes after Booth crossed the bridge, another man approached and spoke with Sgt. Cobb. It was David Herold, however he gave his name as "Smith" to the Army soldier. Cobb once again mentioned the nine PM rule, but Herold gave what seemed to be honest answers and pretended to be unaware of such a law. He alleged his only purpose was to return home to Maryland. Cobb let Herold pass and leave Washington as well. The conspirators, Booth and Herold, met soon after crossing the bridge and traveled together to the Surratt tavern.

The trip was short, but possibly dangerous for John Wilkes Booth. The assassin arrived at the tavern with a broken left leg, the fibula bone to be exact. Scholars and researchers still discuss whether Booth broke his leg from the balcony jump or from a horse accident after crossing the bridge.

The Navy Yard bridge, where Booth and Herold crossed into Maryland.

There is evidence to prove both possibilities, but regardless of where it happened, the injury became a major hindrance in Booth's escape.

After arriving at the tavern, David Herold knocked at the door for tavern keeper John Lloyd. Herold asked for the items that Mary Surratt left for the men earlier that day. Lloyd brought out field glasses and a rifle and noticed Booth on his horse. He offered another rifle to Booth, but the assassin announced that he'd broken his leg and was having enough trouble just staying on the horse. Booth asked Lloyd if any doctors resided in the area, but Lloyd didn't know of any nearby.

The men continued their escape, but traveling through Maryland late at night proved to be torture on John Wilkes Booth. The pain from his broken leg increased as they continued and undoubtedly most of the adrenaline that masked the discomfort earlier in the night had subsided by then. Booth knew of one doctor close enough to help, Dr. Samuel Mudd.

Booth and Mudd met several months earlier on November 13, 1864 near Bryantown, Maryland. Booth needed to buy a horse at the time and a mutual acquaintance introduced the two believing that Mudd had a horse to sell. When it happened that Mudd couldn't sell, he introduced the actor to a horse trader in the area.

Booth and Mudd met a couple other times, a month later, in Washington and were seen with fellow Lincoln kidnapping conspirator John Surratt. The exact details of these meetings is unclear. Most researchers believe them to be accidental encounters, while some evidence leans toward Mudd knowing about the kidnapping plot and that he possibly attended meetings with Booth and the other conspirators at additional times. Whether they planned the stop from the beginning or had an impromptu change of course, John Wilkes Booth and David Herold arrived at Dr. Mudd's home near four AM on April 15. Later, under investigation, Mudd claimed he didn't realize who Booth was for days. A fact investigators found to be a troubling detail.

> ## Assassination Questions
>
> **How did John Wilkes Booth break his leg?**
>
> While most believe Booth broke his leg leaping the twelve feet from the State box to the stage, author Michael Kaufman, in *American Brutus*, argues that Booth actually broke his leg later that night on route to the Surratt tavern. Kaufman believes Booth could not have escaped if the broken leg occurred during the jump and thinks a fall from his horse between the Navy Yard bridge and the tavern caused Booth's broken leg.
>
>

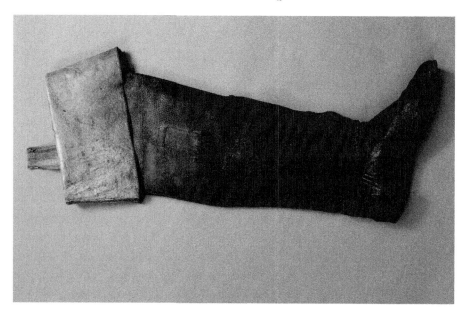

The boot which belonged to John Wilkes Booth. Dr. Mudd had to cut the boot off in order to mend Booth's broken leg.

When Mudd opened the front door to his home, David Herold stood at the threshold. Booth remained on his horse in the distance.[12] Herold informed Mudd that his friend needed a doctor, stating the friend broke his leg from a horse accident. Mudd agreed to help and the two men carried Booth into the house, then upstairs to an empty bed.

After laying Booth down, Mudd examined his left leg and found the boot had to be cut off due to swelling. He sliced the boot material and slid it off, discovering Booth's broken fibula. The bone had broken clean and the overall damage was minimal. With time, his leg would heal without issue and the doctor made a quick splint to immobilize it and lessen the pain. With his work complete, Mudd and Herold left John Wilkes Booth to rest in the upstairs bedroom.

As John Wilkes Booth recovered at the home of Dr. Mudd, back at the Petersen house everyone awaited Abraham Lincoln's impending death. The President's body held out heroically longer than many expected and in the words of Surgeon General Joseph K. Barnes he "showed most wonderful tenacity of life."[13] Despite the unconscious effort of Lincoln's will to survive, the end was not far off.

Throughout the evening and into the early morning of April 15, 1865, the entire cabinet came to visit the dying President. Except for Seward, who was recuperating from his own attack, each man, ally and enemy offered their condolences and came to witness the tragedy with their own eyes. The reactions varied from stoic to sobbing tears, but every one of them understood great changes were to come.

Henry Rathbone left soon after the party arrived at the Petersen house. His valiant effort to ignore his wound and leave all attention on President Lincoln caught up with him quickly. He leaned against the foyer wall but the loss of blood caused him to faint to the floor. Rathbone awakened moments later and Washington D.C. Provost Marshall, General James R. O'Beirne put him into a carriage.

Arriving back at the home of his stepfather Ira Harris, Rathbone's wounds were treated by family doctor G.W. Pope. The doctor noted, after investigating Rathbone's wound, that the blade of the dagger came within one-third of an inch from the brachial artery and deep basilica vein. Had these vessels been cut, the Major would have "bled to death in about five minutes."[14]

In the back parlor of the Petersen house, Secretary of War Edwin Stanton began the investigation of Lincoln's assassins. Stanton interviewed witnesses by the dozen and took statements from investigators and police officers. Other than telegraphs and government officials, he completely shut off Washington from the outside world, no one could enter or exit without permission. The hunt for the men involved with attacks on Lincoln and Seward was in full bloom.

Due to his popularity on stage, many quickly identified John Wilkes Booth as Lincoln's assassin. Several in the audience recognized him instantly, in addition to the actors and stagehands who saw him cross the stage after the gunshot. Unfortunately for Stanton, Booth vanished with little trace of the direction he headed.

Stanton also faced the hurdle of the barrage facts and rumors swirling

Surgeon General Joseph K. Barnes

around Washington. Despite the falsehoods, he quickly gleaned that the orchestrated attacks on Lincoln and Secretary Seward culminated from the work of multiple conspirators. He knew the main fugitive was Booth, but the others involved plagued the Secretary of War.

Stanton's attention alternated from the investigation proceedings in the parlor to the back bedroom, where he kept a close eye on the

Secretary of War Edwin M. Stanton.

> ### Did You Know?
>
> #### The contents of Lincolns Pockets
>
> After Lincoln's death, they found the following items inside his pockets: two pairs of spectacles and a lens polisher, a pocketknife, a watch fob, a linen handkerchief, and a brown leather wallet containing a five-dollar Confederate note and nine newspaper clippings, including several favorable to the president and his policies. Given to his son Robert Todd Lincoln after the assassination, the items are now on display at the Library of Congress.
>
>

President's status. Mary Todd Lincoln did the same, restlessly moving from the front parlor to the back bedroom, escorted by her son Robert. The pain was overwhelming for the soon-to-be widow and wails promptly followed each time she looked up on her slain husband. This occurred several times throughout night, once forcing Stanton to have her removed from the bedroom.

As the late night turned to early morning, the sunrise battled a dreary rainy morning in Washington. Robert tirelessly sat by his mother's side, while young Tad slept at the White House. Lincoln's youngest son never visited the Petersen house that night. As President Lincoln's life was all but over, he lay surrounded by his political allies and enemies, his friends and foes, and his family. Just as he had in life, his death too brought together men of differing opinion for a single cause.

The President's breaths were few and far between by then, and his

Secretary of War Edwin M. Stanton.

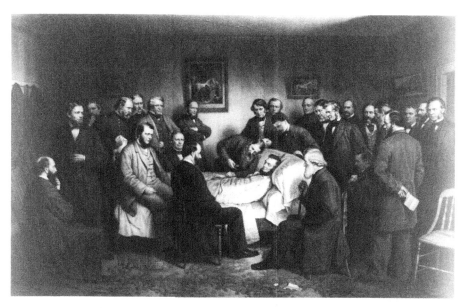

Two depictions of back bedroom of the Petersen house. The room was crowded with guests and visistors throughout the long night.

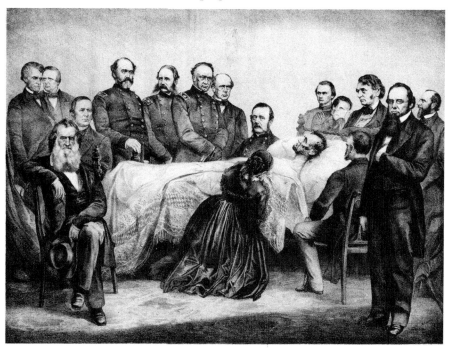

Assassination Questions

Ages or Angels?

Upon Lincoln's death, the Secretary of War is often quoted as saying, "Now he belongs to the ages." This quote of Stanton is often linked to the memories of Lincoln Secretary John Hay, who was also in the room. Dr. Charles Taft, also present at Lincoln's death, remembered Stanton saying "ages" as well. On the opposite side of this discussion, is James Tanner. Tanner was in the Petersen house throughout the night writing shorthand for assassination witness accounts. He recalled Stanton saying, "Now he belongs to the Angels." With differing accounts, this anecdote is one additional item to the list of debated facts by historians and researchers.

The room where Abraham Lincoln died.

pulse could not be found. After quickly confirming with one another, the doctor's agreed and at exactly 7:22 AM they pronounced Abraham Lincoln dead. Some of the men began to weep, while others pondered pensively. Secretary of War Stanton set the stage for Lincoln's impending martyrdom and legend by declaring, "Now he belongs to the ages."

Chapter 6
SEARCH FOR THE MURDERER

On the morning of Abraham Lincoln's death, John Wilkes Booth rested and recovered from his broken leg at the home of Dr. Samuel Mudd. As Booth slept in an upstairs bedroom, his traveling partner David Herold enjoyed breakfast with the doctor. Herold worried about Booth handling the long and arduous trip ahead of them and asked Mudd if he had a carriage to spare. Mudd didn't, but he mentioned that his father may. Mudd planned to head to Bryantown later that day and he decided they could stop by his father's along the way to ask.

Herold left Booth to recuperate and rode with Mudd to his father's home to enquire about the transportation. His father resolutely answered no. With Easter Sunday being the next day, his father intended to use the only carriage he owned for the family to attend church.[15] With no other alternative, Herold decided to leave Mudd and return to the home to retrieve Booth. Mudd continued on to Bryantown without Herold, to pick up his supplies.

In Bryantown, Dr. Mudd first heard of Lincoln's assassination. Soldiers in town searched for the attackers and word spread quickly among the citizens, but nothing caused Mudd to believe the two men at his home played any part in the deed. Yet upon stopping at a friend's house on the way home, and discussing the details of the assassination, Mudd began to wonder if the Booth accused of shooting Lincoln was the same Booth that he met months earlier.[16] With this new thought, Mudd rushed home to confront the men. As he approached his house Dr. Mudd found Booth and Herold already on their horses riding down the road in the opposite direction.

> **DID YOU KNOW?**
>
> **Name is Mudd**
>
> The phrase "Your name is mud" is often attributed to the outlash received by Dr. Mudd after helping John Wilkes Booth. However, the phrase and term mud, meant as dope or dolt, was first seen in print in the 1820's and is mostly likely even older than that.

The doctor called out for them and announced his realization of their identities and what they had done. Booth pleaded with Dr. Mudd to not turn them in, which Mudd agreed to, but ordered them to leave immediately. The two conspirators agreed and rode off into the woods. Mudd thought about riding back to town to report the men, but his wife asked him to wait until the morning. The day neared dark by that time and they would all be going to town for Easter in the morning.

The body of Abraham Lincoln was removed from the Petersen house a little before 9 AM, April 15. In a horse drawn hearse, the President's body traveled the short trip down G Street and Pennsylvania Avenue to the White House. Most of Washington at that point was aware of the President's death and onlookers lined the streets to watch a cavalry escort Lincoln's casket. Upon arrival at the White House, the President's casket, wrapped in an American flag, was carried to an upstairs guest room, known as the Prince of Wales room. Today the room is simply known as a private dining room. In this same room, Lincoln's son Willie died three years earlier from typhoid fever. Now the room would serve as the location for Lincoln's upcoming autopsy.

Dr. Edward Curtis and Dr. Janvier Woodward arrived approximately at 11 a.m to perform the autopsy. Surgeon General Joseph K. Barnes and Dr. Robert Stone also attended the procedure, but only as observers. According to Curtis, the room "contained but little furniture; a large heavily curtained bed, a sofa or two, bureau, wardrobe, and chairs comprised all there was. Seated around the room were several general officers and some civilians, silent or conversing in whispers, and to one side, stretched upon a rough framework of boards and covered only with sheets and towels, lay - cold and immovable - what but a few hours before was the soul of a great nation."[17]

After receiving a detailed description of Lincoln's struggle throughout the night from Surgeon General Barnes, the autopsy officially began at 12:10 PM Dr. Curtis and Dr. Woodward began by removing the back part of the skull and slowly extracting pieces of the brain until they found the track of the ball from John Wilkes Booth's pistol. They noted that the projectile passed from the left side of the head, then through the center of the brain and finally lodged a few inches behind the right eye.

Following the path of the bullet, however, did not result in finding the ball itself. To remedy this, the doctors began removing the remaining pieces of brain until the clacking of the lead bullet, as it bounced against an empty basin underneath the men's workspace, broke the silence in the room. Dr. Curtis, noticing the ball, eloquently described the scene as follows: "There it lay upon the white china, a little black mass no

> **DID YOU KNOW?**
>
> **Mary's Autopsy Request**
>
> As Lincoln's autopsy proceeded in the Prince of Wales room, Mary Todd Lincoln mourned in her bedroom across the hall. She later sent in a messenger to interrupt the surgeons and request a lock of her husband's hair. Mary's request was granted and the hair sent back with the messenger.

> **DID YOU KNOW?**
>
> Johnson Takes Office
>
> On the same day as Lincoln's autopsy, Andrew Johnson was officially sworn in as the 17th President of the United States. The ceremony took place in the front parlor of the Kirkwood house.
>
>

bigger than the end of my finger - dull, motionless and harmless, yet the cause of such mighty changes in the world's history as we may perhaps never realize."

With the autopsy complete, Dr. Charles Brown, undertaker for Brown and Alexander, began the process of embalming Abraham Lincoln's body. Once Dr. Brown completed his work, he then prepared the President's body for his funeral and dressed him in the same suit he wore a month earlier, at his Second Presidential Inauguration.

John Wilkes Booth and David Herold spent the evening of April 15, 1865 wandering through the swamps of southern Maryland. Over the next several days Booth and Herold navigated the woods and bogs until they finally crossed the Potomac river on April 23, 1865. The Union

A reward poster.

army and investigators swept the surrounding areas searching for the two fugitives, but with the help of loyal southerners and a little luck the two avoided capture. Despite missing the conspirators, the Union was close on the trail of Booth and Herold.

On April 24, 1865, after desperately searching for a hideout and place of respite, John Wilkes Booth and David Herold came upon the home and farm of Richard Garrett. Turned away at a couple other locations, Garrett took Booth in. Garrett had no knowledge of the true identity of his guest, as Booth stayed on the farm under the guise of a wounded Confederate soldier. Herold left Booth behind at the Garrett farm and continued on with the men that guided them earlier.

The Garretts believed Booth's story the first day and they allowed the assassin to sleep in the house and enjoy dinner with the family. They treated him as a welcomed guest, with little cause for concern. However, later in the day of April 25, news of Lincoln's assassination reached the farm and the oldest of Garrett's sons realized Booth carried two pistols and a knife. Suspicions now swirled among the family that the wounded soldier could indeed be the President's murderer.

Later that evening Herold returned to the Garrett farm after discovering the army was nearby and on their trail. He thought it best to return to Booth and notify him. The two men appeared ragged and tired from their lengthy ordeal. On the run for eleven days, the journey wore thin and Booth's healing leg slowed their escape.

> **DID YOU KNOW?**
>
> The Reward Money
>
> The decision to offer a $100,000 reward for the capture of the assassination conspirators proved to be a poor choice and may have given Booth and Herold more time to escape. With the promise of such a large amount of money, incorrect information and fake tips sent authorities in multiple directions, all of which resulted in dead ends. Booth and Herold were discovered through investigation and interrogation by the U.S. Army and because no information directly led to the capture of the fugitives, no one was entitled to the whole reward. However, despite the reward having no direct impact on the capture of Booth and Herold, many claims were still submitted for the money.
>
> In the end, a committee of claims investigated every single submission for a reward and determined that twenty-three separate payments would be given. After a bill for reward money was created and passed through both the House and Senate, the $100,000 was split up among the twenty-three groups. All twenty-six soldiers of the 16th New York Cavalry that surrounded Booth and Herold at the Garrett Farm, including Boston Corbett, received $1,653.85. Richard Garrett received no reward money or retribution for his help or the loss of his barn.

After Herold's return, the oldest Garrett sons became even more concerned and after some discussion with Booth and Herold, the sons informed the fugitives they were no longer welcome at the Garrett home. As the night drew near, and fearful of theft and their safety, the Garretts asked Booth and Herold to stay in a barn near the house. The family advised that they could sleep there until the morning, but must leave the next day.

Before the next morning could arrive, at approximately 2 AM of April 26, Booth awoke to the sound of Union soldiers surrounding the Garrett's barn. Booth woke Herold and informed him of the soldiers. Herold proposed that they surrender, but Booth refused. The soldiers called out and demanded that Booth come out and yield or they would burn the barn down.

The soldiers impatiently waited as Booth decided whether to surrender or not. Herold and Booth argued back and forth, as Herold wished to leave before the soldiers began burning the barn. As Booth yelled out questions and demands of his own, the soldiers grew nervous, not sure of what to expect. One such soldier was Sergeant Boston Corbett, a thirty-two year old devoutly religious man and veteran of the ending war.

The shadows of Booth and Herold could be seen through the slats of the barn walls. The soldiers carried candles to illuminate the early morning

> **DID YOU KNOW?**
>
> Boston Corbett's Mental Illness
>
> Boston Corbett, the man that shot John Wilkes Booth, was later admitted to an insane asylum. It's thought that his illness came from his years as a hatter and a prolonged exposure to mercury, which was used in the production of felt for hats.

The Search for the Murderer

A depiction of John Wilkes Booth being dragged from the burning barn on the Garrett Farm.

darkness and the time finally came to use them to drive Booth from his hiding place. They lit a pile of hay near the barn wall; the fire grew quickly and engulfed the fugitives. Herold feared for his life more than Booth and announced his surrender. He approached the barn door and the soldiers ordered him to place his hands out first. Those close by yanked Herold from the barn and searched him for weapons.

Booth moved about the inside of the barn. Desperate for a last minute plan, nothing came to him. He clutched his rifle in one hand and a crutch in the other. Sergeant Corbett peered through a barn crack, with a pistol aimed on John Wilkes Booth. As Booth headed for the door, with gun in hand, Corbett took the opportunity and fired his pistol. The bullet struck Booth through the neck, dropping him immediately to the barn floor.

> ### Did You Know?
>
> #### John Wilkes Booth's Diary
>
> After Booth's death, a journal was found on his body containing entries detailing his escape after the assassination. With passages such as "I think I have done well, though I am abandoned, with the Curse of Cain upon me... To night I try to escape these blood hounds once more." Booth struggled to understand why his deed was not more celebrated and why he was "being hunted like a dog." While the diary was not offered as evidence in the 1865 trial of the conspirators, it was discovered once again in 1867. The diary has more than a dozen pages missing, fueling conspiracy theorists for years that the missing pages hold evidence to the truth behind Lincoln's assassination.
>
>

After they heard the gunshot and saw Booth fall, soldiers burst into the flaming barn to pull out Booth's limp body. They took him to the front porch of the Garrett house, where officers assessed his wound. Unsure at first who shot the assassin, Sergeant Corbett spoke up and stated he shot Booth, fearful the fugitive would attempt to shoot his way out. Booth remained on the porch for the next few hours.

A short time after, a doctor arrived on the scene and diagnosed Booth with a spinal cord injury. The injury didn't allow for a quick and painless death. The assassin survived for a few hours, choking on fluids and paralyzed in his own body. He had difficulty clearing his throat and his vital organs began shutting down.[18] At approximately seven o'clock, just after sunrise on April 26, 1865, John Wilkes Booth was pronounced dead.

On April 19, 1865, in the East Room of the White House, the body of Abraham Lincoln laid in an open casket awaiting the day's funeral. A day earlier, an estimated 30,000 visitors passed through the room to pay respects to their slain leader. The 3,200-square-foot room, draped in black cloth, was large but the overwhelming number of visitors caused many to wait between two and six hours to see the President's body.

For the funeral, six hundred invitations had been handed out, and the ticket holders began filtering into the East room just before noon. Upon entering the room, all eyes immediately drew to President Lincoln's coffin sitting upon an enormous catafalque, draped with black and white cloth. Robert and Tad Lincoln sat closest to the coffin along with Lincoln's secretaries John Nicolay and John Hay. Mary Todd Lincoln did not make an appearance. Self-confined to her bedroom, she never attended any funeral for her husband.

With everyone seated, the funeral began a few minutes after noon. Dr. Phineas D. Gurley, the Lincoln family pastor, presided and gave the sermon. Among the six hundred in attendance, General Grant sat near the coffin, opposite Lincoln's sons and secretaries. Lincoln's cabinet members all sat together on one side, with President Andrew Johnson in front and Lincoln's first Vice President Hannibal Hamlin next to him.

After the funeral, President Lincoln's body and coffin were carried to an awaiting horse drawn hearse outside of the White House. From there a funeral procession traveled to the Capitol building which included Union soldiers and approximately 40,000 newly freed blacks holding hands. The sight marveled all in attendance and nearly 100,000

The hearse used to carry the body of President Abraham Lincoln.

people lined the streets to behold their beloved President being laid to rest. With the procession nearly three miles long, it took a little over two hours to pass a specific point. Journalist Ben Perley Poore described the scene as follows:

"At two PM the funeral procession started, all of the bells in the city tolling, and minute guns firing from all the forts. Pennsylvania Avenue, from the Treasury to the Capitol, was entirely clear from curb to curb. Preceding the hearse was the military escort, over one mile long, the arms of each officer and man being draped with black. At short intervals bands discoursed dirges and drums beat muffled sounds. After the artillery came the civic procession, headed by Marshal Lamon, the Surgeon-General, and physicians who attended the President. At this point the hearse appeared, and the thousands, as it passed, uncovered their heads."

The funeral procession for Abraham Lincoln on Pennsylvania Avenue.

Upon arrival at the Capitol, Lincoln's body was moved into the rotunda of the great building and the next day an estimated 25,000 or more visitors viewed the President. Covered with flowers and surrounded by guards, the President was available to all admirers, just as he was in life. Lincoln remained in the Capitol rotunda overnight, waiting for the funeral train arrangements to be completed. The President's body would follow a path similar to the Inaugural train route he rode five years earlier. The body of Lincoln's deceased son, Willie, would accompany him and be buried with his father in Springfield, Illinois.

The funeral train car that carried Abraham Lincoln's body from Washington D.C. to Springfield, Illinois.

The funeral train engine that traveled across the country passing thousands of grieving citizens.

The Search for the Murderer

Above: The funeral procession for Abraham Lincoln in New York - April 25, 1865.
Below: The funeral stop in Chicago, Illinois.

Early in the morning of April 21, the slain President began a journey that included stops in seven states. These states included Maryland, Pennsylvania, New Jersey, New York, Ohio, Indiana, and Illinois. The trip totaled 1700 miles and over the entire journey an estimated thirty million people paid their respects to their beloved Abraham Lincoln. This number doesn't include the thousands unable to view Lincoln's coffin due to the schedule.

After entering Illinois, the train made a stop in Chicago, allowing some 37,000 mourners to pass by the open coffin. The next day, May 3, 1865, in Lincoln's hometown of Springfield, Illinois, the train made its final stop. The heartache felt across the country multiplied in Springfield by the intimacy they shared with Lincoln and the ownership they felt in helping create the national hero. This closeness is well represented in the words of William Henry Herndon, Lincoln's former law partner.

"The funeral train reached Springfield on the 3rd of May. The casket was borne to the State House and placed in Representative Hall – the very chamber in which, in 1854, the deceased had pronounced that fearful invective against the sin

> ### Did You Know?
> #### Robert Lincoln Saved by Edwin Booth
>
> A year or so before the assassination, Robert Todd Lincoln was saved by assassin John Wilkes Booth's brother, Edwin Booth. Standing on a crowded train platform, Robert Lincoln lost his footing as the train next to him began to move. As Lincoln fell off the landing, Edwin grabbed Lincoln's coat collar and pulled him to safety. Robert recognized Edwin and thanked him by name.
>
>

The Search for the Murderer

DID YOU KNOW?

Mary Todd's Stay in the White House

Suffering with major grief and depression after Lincoln's death, Mary Todd refused to leave the White House for five weeks. On May 22, 1865, Mary Todd, accompanied by Robert and Tad, finally left the White House and boarded a train to Illinois.

The home of Abraham Lincoln in Springfield, Illinois, decorated for Lincoln's funeral.

of human slavery. The doors were thrown open, the coffin lid was removed, and we had known the illustrious dead in other days, and before the nation lay its claim upon him, moved sadly through and looked for the last time on the silent, upturned face of our departed friend. All day long and through the night a stream of people filed reverently by the catafalque. Some of them were his colleagues at the bar; some his old friends from New Salem; some crippled soldiers fresh from the battlefields of the war; and some were little children who, scarce realizing the impressiveness of the scene, were destined to live and tell their children yet to be born the sad story of Lincoln's death."[19]

On May 4, 1865, Lincoln's casket was closed for the last time. Never again would anyone look upon the face that carried the United States through the most difficult hardship in its existence. The bodies of Abraham Lincoln and Willie Lincoln were buried in Springfield's Oak Ridge Cemetery. Today, the grave is an Illinois historic site and also holds the remains of Mary Todd Lincoln and their two sons Tad and Edward Lincoln. Robert Todd Lincoln is buried in Arlington National Cemetery.

Chapter 7

THE CONSPIRATORS' TRIAL

After the murder of their beloved leader, the nation demanded quick retribution. Secretary of War Stanton felt the same desire and drove the trial of the conspirators with a determined fervor. He would soon pressure President Andrew Johnson and other officials to keep the trial in the hands of the government and military, giving him more control of the process.

With the hunt for John Wilkes Booth over and David Herold captured, the last of the remaining conspirators had been rounded up and a trial could commence. At the time of Booth's death the U.S. government already had several men and women behind bars they believed to be involved with Lincoln's death. Among the captured, ultimately eight prisoners were tried for Lincoln's murder and their connection to the larger kidnapping conspiracy. The eight included David Herold, Edman "Ned" Spangler, Samuel Arnold, Michael

O'Laughlen, Mary Surratt, Lewis Powell, George Atzerodt, and Dr. Samuel Mudd. Herold joined the others after his capture in Virginia. The hunt still continued for one man, John Surratt, the son of Mary Surratt.

Edman "Ned" Spangler was a carpenter and stagehand at Ford's Theatre. He'd met Booth when they were just young boys in Maryland and many knew him to be an acquaintance of the assassin. The prosecution found little evidence against Spangler and a true connection to the kidnapping conspiracy has never been found.

Spangler appeared to be a sad looking fellow and was described as having an "unintelligent-looking face... swollen by the excessive use of alcohol, a low forehead, brown hair, and anxious-looking eyes."[20] Regardless of his appearance, Spangler was a competent carpenter and scene shifter at Ford's Theatre. On the night of the assassination, Booth had called for Spangler to come hold his horse in the alley behind the theater. Spangler had reluctantly accepted the task as Booth stormed away, but he relinquished it to another stagehand, Joseph

> **DID YOU KNOW?**
>
> Robert Lincoln at all the Assassinations
>
> In addition to being in Washington during his father's assassination, Robert was also present for the assassinations of Presidents James A. Garfield and William McKinley. When Garfield was shot in a D.C. train station in 1881, Lincoln, serving as Garfield's Secretary of War, was in the crowd awaiting the train to New Jersey with the President. Finally, in 1901, serving as President of the Pullman Company, Lincoln attended the Pan-American Exhibition in Buffalo, New York at the same time as President McKinley. Lincoln was on his way to meet McKinley when the assassination occurred.

The Conspirators' Trial

Assassination Questions

Was Edman "Ned" Spangler a true conspirator?

Of all the conspirators involved in Lincoln's assassination, Spangler's guilt is the most questionable. Labeled by many as a quiet and simple man, Spangler may have lacked any skills Booth found necessary for the plot. Doomed by his acquaintance with the assassin and possibly false evidence against him, Spangler was possibly most guilty of simple association. On the night of assassination, when Booth demanded he hold the escape horse, Spangler's devotion was to the theater. This was not the action of a man involved in an organized conspiracy. Upon Spangler's death, a note found inside his tool chest, detailed his relationship with Booth. In the note, Spangler stated, "I never heard Booth express himself in favor of the rebellion, or opposed to the Government, or converse upon political subjects; and I have no recollection of his mentioning the name of President Lincoln in any connection whatever. I know nothing of the mortise hole said to be in the wall behind the door of the President's box, or of any wooden bar to fasten or hold the door being there, or of the lock being out of order. I did not notice any hole in the door."[21]

Did You Know?

The Contents of Booth's Wallet and Pockets

After John Wilkes Booth's death, five pictures of women were found, among a dozen other items. The images were of his fiancée Lucy Hale and actresses Alice Grey, Helen Western, Effie Germon, and Fanny Brown. While Booth was known as a ladies man, he devoted much of his time to Hale. She was the daughter of New Hampshire Senator John Parker Hale and a sought after woman with many admirers. The couple was secretly engaged in early 1865, but Booth and Senator Hale were on opposite sides of the slavery debate. Lucy and her family lived in the National Hotel, where Booth also stayed while in Washington. After the assassination, Lucy moved to Spain with her father, where he took up the position of U.S. Ambassador.

"Peanuts" Burroughs. Burroughs actually held the horse later that night before Booth escaped from Ford's. Despite this little involvement, Spangler was ultimately undone by the evidence of Jacob Ritterspaugh, another Ford's stagehand. Ritterspaugh testified in court that Spangler hit him in the face and demanded him not to say which way Booth escaped.

The next two men, Samuel Arnold and Michael O'Laughlen had been in custody nearly as long as Spangler. All three men were taken on April 17, nine days before Booth would be killed. Arnold and O'Laughlen had both been involved with the original kidnapping plot, but lost interest as the months progressed and the war seemed to be coming to an end. Booth did speak with O'Laughlen the morning of the assassination, but ultimately left him out of the final plans that night to assassinate the three leaders- Lincoln, Johnson, and Seward.

Mary Surratt and Lewis Powell were taken into custody later the same night. Investigators received information that several of the conspirators had been meeting at the Surratt boarding house at 541 H Street in Washington. In addition to this, John Surratt's name appeared in multiple reports as an acquaintance of John Wilkes Booth.

Investigators arrived on the night of April 17 at the Surratt boarding house to question Mary Surratt and attempt to locate her son, John. The authorities searched the house and informed Mary Surratt of her arrest. During this process Lewis Powell arrived at the home carrying a pickaxe. Powell's appearance at such a late hour, around midnight, confused and alerted the investigators. Powell announced that Surratt hired him to dig a drain and he arrived late in order to find out where she needed the work; this way he could begin the next morning. Mary Surratt denied knowing Powell, a fact that would later hurt her in court, but her denial failed to convince the investigators and they arrested Powell that night as well.

George Atzerodt, the man Booth tasked with killing Vice President Johnson, was arrested on April 20. Involved from the beginning, Atzerodt abandoned his duty on assassination night and fled from the National Hotel. Authorities found him three days later on a Maryland farm and brought him in for questioning.

The case against Dr. Mudd was fraught with complications. The doctor had been introduced to Booth months earlier in 1864, however his involvement in the kidnapping plot has never been proven. Mudd's first meeting with Booth revolved around the soon to be assassin's search for a horse and possibly buying land in Maryland. Mudd was seen in the company of Booth a second time in December of 1864 at the National Hotel. During this meeting, witness Louis J. Wiechmann noted that he accompanied John Surratt when Dr. Mudd introduced Surratt to John Wilkes Booth. The men discussed several topics in a room at the National Hotel, one of which involved the roads in Charles County, Maryland; possibly planning Booth's escape from Washington.

In addition to Mudd's previous involvement with Booth, the doctor's changing story, when questioned by investigators, proved detrimental. After setting Booth's broken leg during his escape, Mudd alerted the soldiers in nearby Bryantown that he believed the two men at his home were Booth and Herold, however he informed the authorities he'd never met the assassin. Mudd's account of his interaction with the fugitives didn't sit well with the investigators and caused them to return multiple times to Mudd's farm. On the second occasion they informed Mudd that his home would be searched and upon notification of this Mudd informed them that he found a boot recently and believed it to be Booth's. The investigators examined the cut boot and found an inscription inside which read, "J. Wilkes." After further questioning and confirmation with officers in charge of the conspiracy investigation, Mudd was arrested the and taken to

> ### Did You Know?
>
> The Collapse of Ford's Theatre
>
> The Ford's Theatre standing today is not the same one Abraham Lincoln visited in 1865. On June 9, 1893, the theater collapsed, killing twenty-two people. Used as a military office building at the time, the accident occurred after a basement support beam broke. The theater was rebuilt and used by the Government Printing Office until 1931. In 1932, Ford's Theatre became a National Historic site and renovations were made to return it to it's 1865 appearance. In 1968, the theater opened as a functioning theater and museum.

Washington.

Before the trial against the conspirators could begin, the type of trial, civil or military, needed to be determined. The accused could be tried

David Herold.

Lewis Powell.

George Atzerodt.

Samuel Arnold.

Michael O'Laughlin.

Edman Spangler.

Dr. Samuel Mudd.

Library of Congress, Prints & Photographs Division, NYWT&S Collection, [reproduction number, e.g., LC-USZ62-111157]

Mary Surratt.

in a civil court. But because the defendants could be deemed as spies during a time of war and they committed the act of the murder of a President, in a location where martial law existed, they could be also tried by a military tribunal. The tribunal would give the government more control and quicker justice. Some did fear that putting the fate of the conspirators into the hands of the public would lengthen the process and allow opinions a greater opportunity to sway a jury. With Stanton's case argued and grounded in precedent with legal justification, President Andrew Johnson declared the conspirators would be tried by a Military Commission on May 1, 1865.

> **DID YOU KNOW?**
>
> No Pictures, Please
>
> Several mugshots of the six conspirators (Powell, Herold, Azterodt, Spangler, Arnold, and O'Laughlen) exist because their photos were taken while imprisoned on the monitors. Mugshots of Mary Surratt and Dr. Samuel Mudd do not exist from these photo sessions because they were never held on the monitors. While the others were prime suspects, Surratt and Mudd didn't become official suspects until later and were held in the arsenal prison.

At this time, seven of the eight prisoners found themselves held in the federal penitentiary in Washington D.C., near the Potomac and Anacostia rivers. Today it's the site of the U.S. Army base Fort McNair. Dr. Samuel Mudd joined his fellow conspirators a few days later on May 4. John Frederick Hartranft, special provost marshal and military governor of the Washington Arsenal, acted as guard and kept watch over the prisoners.

Hartranft's duties included feeding and cleaning the Lincoln conspirators, in addition to handling their communication with outside visitors and legal representation. Their meals consisted of mostly bread, salt meat, and coffee, and each prisoner had their own cell, preventing them from speaking to one another. He also arranged their physical examinations daily to verify their health.

Prior to the federal penitentiary, most of the accused awaited their fate on the monitor ships Saugus and Montauk. Monitors were warships used during the Civil War and carried large guns. They allowed for

Gen. John F. Hartranft and staff's duties included securing the conspirators at the Arsenal.

travel down shallow rivers and bombardment of enemy forces. During their times on the monitors, officers forced the conspirators to wear hoods covering their entire heads. Used as a way to disorient them and keep them from understanding their location, the prisoners wore the hoods at all times except when eating. This practice continued even after transfer to the federal penitentiary, where they required all but Surratt and Mudd to wear them. In addition to the hoods, all prisoners wore shackles around their wrists and ankles. Powell and Atzerodt had a large iron ball added to their shackles.

The conspirators spent a rather uneventful time in prison, other than Mary Surratt's refusal to eat for several days and Powell smashing the iron ball, attached to his leg, against his head. Officers removed the iron balls from both Powell and Atzerodt after that incident. In addition, in early June, they removed the hoods from the all the prisoners, except Powell. According to Hartranft, Powell didn't seem to "suffer as much

The Conspirators' Trial   113

The board which tried the Conspirators.
Standing left to right: Brig. Gen. Thomas M. Harris, Maj. Gen. Lew Wallace, Maj. Gen. August V. Kautz, and Henry L. Burnett. Seated left to right: Lt. Col. David R. Clendenin, Col. C.H. Tompkins, Brig. Gen. Albion P. Howe, Brig. Gen. James Ekin, Maj. Gen. David Hunter, Brig. Gen. Robert S. Foster, John A. Binham, and Brig. Gen. Joseph Holt.

as the others and there may be some necessity for his wearing it."[22]

On May 12, 1865, the trial of the conspirators began and testimony against the accused was heard. The trial took place in the Old Arsenal Building, near the federal prison. Many of the prisoners chose their own legal representation, while the court offered lawyers for the poorer conspirators. The trial took place before a military tribunal of nine men, including a mixture of colonels and generals.

The conspirators had only been advised of the charges against them a few days prior on May 8. Hartranft personally delivered the charges to each prisoner: conspiracy to "kill and murder" the President of the United States.[23] On May 10, officers brought each prisoner to the courtroom individually and the judge read them the charges. Afterwards, each one plead "Not Guilty."

The trial lasted a total of 48 days, ending on June 29, 1865. The details of the conspiracy to kidnap and the plot that resulted in

Lewis Powell.

The Conspirators' Trial

Lincoln's murder had been investigated from every angle. In total, the prosecution and defense called upon the testimony of 366 witnesses. The major conspirators, including Powell, Atzerodt, and Herold, were doomed from the start. However, the others soon learned that their guilt lay in the fact that, despite not cooperating in the later murder plot, simply knowing about the plot in the first place and their lack of any attempt to stop it, made them guilty. This is known as vicarious liability.

After all evidence had been heard, the tribunal deliberated a verdict and penalty for each. The court ordered Hartranft to deliver the verdicts in person. On July 6, he visited the cells of Lewis Powell, George Atzerodt, David Herold, and Mary Surratt to inform them that they had been found guilty and would be put to death by hanging. The other four prisoners, Mudd, Arnold, O'Laughlen, and Spangler had also been found guilty but the tribunal spared them the death penalty. They did not learn of this information until July 17. Out of the four men, only Spangler did not receive a life term. The tribunal ordered him to serve only six years in prison. They would all serve their sentences in Fort Jefferson, an island prison in the Florida Keys.

On July 7, 1865, George Atzerodt, Mary Surratt, Lewis Powell, and David Herold were escorted from their cells to the prison yard of the Arsenal Penitentiary. It was a hot day and the guards brought the prisoners out a little after noon. They fitted each with hanging caps, guided the four conspirators up the steps of the temporary gallows, and positioned them into place in front of one of the four nooses. A trap door under each noose would fall upon orders, allowing the body to drop.

In front of the gallows, a group, numbering nearly a thousand, waited patiently under the hot summer sun to see the conspirators hang. The crowd consisted mostly of military personnel and reporters, but did include some family and friends of the condemned. Underneath the gallows, soldiers positioned themselves near the supporting poles which held the trap doors closed.

With everyone in place, officials gave the signal at 1:26 PM The soldiers underneath removed the supporting poles and the bodies of Atzerodt, Surratt, Powell, and Herold fell through the trap doors. They

The execution of the conspirators. Temporary gallows were built in the prison yard. Image taken from the roof of the Arsenal.

Moments before the hanging. The ropes being adjusted to fit the conspirators.

The Conspirators' Trial

Above: The trap doors opened and the conspirators hanging.
Below: Coffins and open graves prepared for the bodies.

fell approximately five to six feet and the bodies rested in place for the next twenty-five minutes, giving ample time to ensure official death. Around 2 PM soldiers cut the bodies down, laid them in coffins with their hanging caps on, and physicians examined them to verify death. They buried all four conspirators in pre-dug graves next to the gallows.

After the hangings, Secretary Stanton and much of the public felt some retribution took place. The majority of those involved were either dead or on their way to prison. The only man to escape full punishment was John Surratt. He wouldn't be captured for another nineteen months after traveling to Egypt and being recognized by officials. In 1867, Surratt was tried before a civilian court. It ended in a mistrial and they set John Surratt free.

With their fellow prisoners deceased, the four men who escaped

John Surratt - Son of Mary Surratt.

Did You Know?

Fort Jefferson and the Dry Tortugas

After the assassination trial, Edman Spangler, Dr. Samuel Mudd, Michael O'Laughlin, and Samuel Arnold were all sentenced to serve time at Fort Jefferson, a military fort turned prison in the Dry Tortugas off the coast of Florida. The 73 square mile island lies seventy miles west of Key West and today operates as a National Park for tourists. The four conspirators never served their full sentences after President Andrew Johnson pardoned them all in 1869.

the gallows, Spangler, Mudd, Arnold, and O'Laughlin, started their sentence in Fort Jefferson on July 24, 1865. The men suffered many ordeals in Fort Jefferson with the worst of them being an epidemic of yellow fever in 1867. Both prisoners and guards came down with the viral disease which caused such symptoms as fever, chills, headaches, bleeding from the eyes and mouth, and vomiting blood. With no one else to turn to, Fort Jefferson officials asked Dr. Mudd to assist with treating guards and prisoners. Of the three Lincoln conspirators, the disease only took the life of Michael O'Laughlin. The others flirted with the illness, but survived to see their freedom.

In the spring of 1869, President Andrew Johnson pardoned all three Lincoln prisoners. He pardoned Mudd first, followed a few weeks later by Spangler and O'Laughlin. Mudd traveled back to his farm in Maryland to be with his family. After returning, he tried his hand in local politics, found some small success, but failed to achieve any great notoriety. In 1883, at the age of forty-nine, Dr. Samuel Mudd died of pneumonia.

Spangler went back to carpentry, but found himself on the Mudd farm not long after, where he did odd jobs and lived in a small building on Mudd's property. Spangler lived only six years after his release from prison, dying February 7, 1875, from a respiratory ailment. He was buried near Mudd's farm.

Samuel Arnold lived a relatively quiet life after his release from Fort Jefferson. His name showed up briefly in 1902 after writing a series of newspaper articles in the *Baltimore American*, describing his involvement in the Lincoln assassination and his time at Fort Jefferson. He died September 21, 1902, at the age of seventy-two.

Conclusion

In the history of the United States there are few tragedies that equal the gravitas of the assassination of Abraham Lincoln. Becoming the first murdered President in the country's existence catapulted an already legendary leader into a mythical hero revered for his determination and foresight. A martyr for his cause, Lincoln still stands as a symbol of change one-hundred-fifty years after his death, and the uniqueness of his qualities has yet to be matched.

While history may have heightened the truth of who Abraham Lincoln was, through embellishment and folklore, the foundation of the great politician and leader he was cannot be argued. In addition, the theatrics, drama, and ultimately vague aspects of his death even further expands the narrative on Honest Abe.

The mystery of the assassination, including both the cold hard facts and the malleable eyewitness accounts, never fails to excite. New audiences and researchers, in the trenches of assassination lore for years, continue to dissect the facts. As new data, information, and theories pop up periodically, it's churned through a rigorous vetting process before being ultimately accepted into the traditional account of assassination.

This book, meant to be a primer for further research and discussion, is simply one more addition into the cavalcade of books, magazines, and essays on the topic of Abraham Lincoln and his murder. With the ultimate goal of reaching a wider audience to inspire the minds of future investigators, teachers, and history enthusiasts, what better tool to use than Abraham Lincoln. A man that time after time is

Conclusion

consistently ranked as the greatest U.S. President. A man who gave his life to keep what he deemed the greatest country in the world united. A man who believed in the law and democracy. And a man who had the courage to finally abolish slavery and begin the process of removing the stain of America's most inhuman period.

References

1. Holzer, Harold. *The President Is Shot!: The Assassination of Abraham Lincoln.* Honesdale, PA: Boyds Mills, 2004. Page 50.

2. SEWARD, William Henry., and Frederick William. SEWARD. *William H. Seward: An Autobiography ... With a Memoir ... by F.W. Seward. (Seward at Washington as Senator and Secretary of State ... by F.W. Seward.).* 3 Vol. Derby and Miller: New York, 1891. Page 275.

3. Welles, Gideon, Edgar Thaddeus Welles, and John T. Morse. *Diary of Gideon Welles: Secretary of the Navy under Lincoln and Johnson. Vol. II.* Boston: Houghton Mifflin, 1911. Pages 280-283.

4. Bates, David Homer. *Lincoln in the Telegraph Office; Recollections of the United States Military Telegraph Corps during the Civil War.* New York: Century, 1907. Pages 366-368.

5. Booth, John Wilkes, John H. Rhodehamel, and Louise Taper. *Right or Wrong, God Judge Me: The Writings of John Wilkes Booth.* Urbana: U of Illinois, 1997. Pages 151-152.

6. Rathbone, Henry. *Interview with A.B. Olin. Reminiscences and Souvenirs of the Assassination of Abraham Lincoln.* Washington: Press of Rufus H. Darby, 1894. Pages 73-76.

7. IBID

8. IBID

9. "Report of Dr. Charles A. Leale on Assassination, April 15, 1865." *Report of Dr. Charles A. Leale on Assassination, April 15, 1865. The Papers of Abraham Lincoln*, 2012. Web. 06 Apr. 2015. Record Group 112: Office of the Surgeon General (War), 1775-1959, Entry 12, Letters Received, 1818-1889, National Archives Building, Washington, DC

10. Testimony of Dr. Robert King Stone, 5/16/1865, Records of the Office of the Judge Advocate General (Army), National Archives Identifier: 784372

11. Shea, John Gilmary. *The Lincoln Memorial: A Record of the Life, Assassination, and Obsequies of the Martyred President.* New York: Bunce and Huntington, 1865. Page 69.

12. Kauffman, Michael W. "Twelve - Sic Semper Tyrannis." *American Brutus: John Wilkes Booth and the Lincoln Conspiracies.* New York: Random House, 2004

13. Goldstein, Richard. *Mine Eyes Have Seen: A First Person History of the Events That Shaped America.* New York: Simon & Schuster, 1997. Page 118.

14. "President Lincoln - The Tragedy." *The Public Ledger* [Philadelphia] 5 May 1865: n. pag. *The Public Ledger* - May 5, 1865. Web. 11 Aug. 2010.

15. Kauffman, Michael W. "Thirteen - I Believe He Would Have Murdered Us, Every One." *American Brutus: John Wilkes Booth and the Lincoln Conspiracies.* New York: Random House, 2004.

16. IBID

17. "Was At the Lincoln Autopsy." *The Reading Eagle* [Reading, Penn-

sylvania] 19 Apr. 1903: 8. Web. 10 May 2014. <https://news.google.com/newspapers?nid=1955&dat=19030419&id=RRYrAAAAIBAJ&sjid=zpwFAAAAIBAJ&pg=4954,4888659&hl=en>.

18. Kauffman, Michael W. "Fifteen - I Must Fight The Course." *American Brutus: John Wilkes Booth and the Lincoln Conspiracies*. New York: Random House, 2004.

19. Herndon, William Henry, and David Freeman. Hawke. *Herndon's Lincoln; the True Story of a Great Life*. Vol. 3. Indianapolis: Bobbs-Merrill, 1970.

20. Poore, Benjamin Perley. *The Conspiracy Trial for the Murder of the President, and the Attempt to Overthrow the Government by the Assassination of Its Principal Officers*. New York: Arno, 1972.

21. Mudd, Samuel Alexander, and Nettle Mudd. *The Life of Dr. Samuel A. Mudd; Containing His Letters from Fort Jefferson, Dry Tortugas Island, Where He Was Imprisoned Four Years for Alleged Complicity in the Assassination of Abraham Lincoln, with Statements of Mrs. Samuel A. Mudd, Dr. Samuel A. Mudd, and Edward Spangler regarding the Assassinatin and the Argument of General Ewing on the Question of the Jurisdiction of the Military Commission, and on the Law and Facts of the Case; Also "diary" of John Wilkes Booth*. New York and Washington: Neale Pub., 1906.

22. Hartranft, John F., Edward Steers, and Harold Holzer. *The Lincoln Assassination Conspirators: Their Confinement and Execution, as Recorded in the Letterbook of John Frederick Hartranft*. Baton Rouge: Louisiana State UP, 2009. Page 43.

23. Steers, Edward. *The Trial: The Assassination of President Lincoln and the Trial of the Conspirators*. Lexington, KY: U of Kentucky, 2003

Printed in Great Britain
by Amazon